The Tao and Mother Goose

Cover Art:
Aphrodite on a Goose, terra cotta sculpture from Boetia, Classical Period. Photo courtesy of Princeton University Press.

THE TAO AND MOTHER GOOSE

Robert Carter

*This publication made possible with
the assistance of the Kern Foundation*

**The Theosophical Publishing House
Wheaton, Ill. U.S.A.
Madras, India/London, England**

The Theosophical Publishing House
306 West Geneva Road
Wheaton, IL 60187
A publication of the Theosophical Publishing House, a depart-
ment of the Theosophical Society in America.

Library of Congress Cataloging in Publication Data

Carter, Robert, 1939-
The Tao and Mother Goose.

  (A Quest book)
  "A Quest original"-T.p. verso.
  Bibliography: p.
  1. Lao-tzu. Tao te ching.   2. Nursery rhymes--
History and criticism.   I. Title.
BL1900.L35C37   1988   299'.51482   87-40524
ISBN 0-8356-0631-7

Printed in the United States of America

Contents

Preface, ix

Acknowledgements, xv

I   The Tao, 1

II   The Mother, 21

III   Mother Goose, 35
      The Goose, 45

IV   Myth and Meaning, 55
      Rhyme and Reason, 63

V   The Rhymes, 73
      Hush a by, Baby: The Tree of Life
        and Death, 75
      Humpty Dumpty and The Cosmic
        Egg, 85
      Mary had a little lamb: A Song of
        Innocence, 96
      Little Bo-peep and *Wu Wei*, 103
      Little Boy Blue: The Divine
        Child, 110
      Peter, his Pumpkin and his
        Wives, 116
      Jack and Jill and Yin and Yang, 123

VI   Monsters and Heroes, 133
        The Monster, 138
        The Divine Fool, 150
        Teachings of The Divine Fool, 163

VII Summary and Conclusion, 169

    Notes, 181

Illustrations

Symbol of the Tao, ink painting by the author, 2

Venus of Willendorf, c. 16,000-10,000 B.C., Museum of Natural History, Vienna, 22

Mother Goose, from *The Real Mother Goose,* by Blanche Fisher Wright, 36

Wild Goose, ink painting by Mu Ch'i, 13th century China, Berlin Ostasiatisches Museum, 44

Brahma on a Cosmic Gander, painting from southern India, 48

Papyrus of Tameniu, 21st Dynasty Egypt, 50

Aphrodite riding on a goose, line drawing by the author, after Pistoxenus, painter, Attic cup, Greece, 500-475 B.C. (British Museum), 52

The wak-wak tree with its human fruit, from *A Turkish History of the West Indies,* Constantinople, 1730, 77

Yakshi figure, from East gate, Great Stupa, Sanchi, India, 80

Prajapati with the world-egg, India, from
Müller, *Glauben, Wissen und Kunst der alten
Hindus,* Mainz, 1822, 89

Lamb of God, carved stone panel, chapel at
Benoit-sur-Loire, 98

Peter, Pumpkin Eater, from *The Real Mother
Goose,* by Blanche Fisher Wright, 117

Kali, copper sculpture, southern India, 19th
century, 136

Daruma, ink painting by Sesshu (A.D.
1420-1506), Japan, 159

Hyonen Zu (catfish and gourd), ink painting
by Josetsu (active c. 1400 A.D.), Japan, 162

Preface

IT IS CLEAR from the title that this book is
concerned with two utterly disparate literary
sources. One is an Eastern collection of ancient rhymes, grouped under the title *Tao Teh
Ching*. And the other is a Western collection
of much less ancient rhymes, collectively
known as the rhymes of Mother Goose. On
the face of it, there would hardly seem to be
two subjects less alike.

The *Tao Teh Ching* dates back to the sixth
century before Christ, and was reputedly
written by Lao Tsu, a real or perhaps fictional and symbolic figure, depending upon
which scholarly view is adopted. For our pur-
poses, it makes little difference. The book is
available in a number of very different translations into English, and consists of roughly
five thousand words, arranged in eighty-one
verses or chapters. Most translations devote
far more space to interpretation and commentary than to the verses themselves.

It is a religious or philosophical as well as a
poetic work. Above all else, it describes the
Tao, which is most often translated *"The
Way."* But there is really no single appropriate English word for *Tao*. It might be

called "God," but that would be misleading, or "the will of God," or "Godhead," which might be less so but which are still unsatisfactory.

Along with the *Upanishads* of the Indian tradition, the *Tao Teh Ching* may well represent one of the most remarkable literary examples of Eastern mysticism. It is simple, brief, cryptic, and profound.

The rhymes of Mother Goose are simple, brief, and often cryptic as well, to the point of being non-sensible, or perhaps just nonsensical. There are at least two hundred or so of these traditional rhymes, some extremely well known and others less so, and for the most part their authors are unknown. We will deal at some length with only a few of the very best known rhymes, and will suggest not only that these have a certain hidden profundity, but that, in their way, they treat religious and philosophical themes similar in many respects to those of the *Tao Teh Ching*. It is admittedly an unusual premise.

In a sense, however, this book is *not* concerned with either the *Tao Teh Ching* or the rhymes of Mother Goose. Certainly it is not concerned with Taoism, the historical Chinese religion, and it is not concerned with the historical origins and setting which produced the *Tao Teh Ching*. Neither will it attempt any extensive argument, commentary, or interpretation of the rhymes.

The book is equally unconcerned with the literary and historical origins of the various Mother Goose rhymes which will be examined, though naturally some attention must be paid these. Neither is it concerned with the scholarly attempts at tracing the historical derivations of the figure of Mother Goose, though this subject requires some brief attention as well.

Dozens of scholars have written exhaustively and well about all of these things, and anyone interested in literary critiques or historical and scholarly analyses of either of the two subjects has a wealth of published material from which to choose.

Perhaps it would be most accurate to say simply that this book is concerned with the same things which seem to concern the *Tao Teh Ching* and these selected rhymes of Mother Goose. The book is not *about* the *Tao Teh Ching* or the rhymes of Mother Goose. Rather it is *about what they are about*. That is a subtle, but necessary and accurate distinction.

The *Tao Teh Ching*, in its historical context, was ostensibly directed at a hypothetical ruler, and instructed him in how to rule and how to use his powers. In a philosophical and religious context, of course, it is a great deal more than that, and is directed at any audience that shares its intense preoccupation with the ''secret'' of existence.

Of the two hundred and more rhymes of

Mother Goose, some few apparently originated as bits of derisive doggerel aimed at public figures, and as such were intended for adults. Most of the rhymes, however, were directed at an audience of young children, and were meant to entertain and to instruct them in a number of different ways, about important and unimportant things.

In a philosophical, or perhaps a psychological context, they may be a great deal more than that, and may contain some hidden lessons that are valuable for adults as well— particularly for the adult who is attracted by the kinds of concerns and teachings in the *Tao Teh Ching*.

This book is meant as an interpretive meditation, and is thus naturally prey to as much critical misgiving and skepticism as anyone may wish to bring to its reading. It is entirely possible that the unknown authors of the nursery rhymes discussed here had no understanding or intent even remotely like that which will be ascribed to their rhymes, and that they might disagree completely with the interpretations. But that may not matter so very much after all. The truth of an idea cannot be confined to the circumstances of its origin. Occasionally we all speak more than we know, and so it may matter less where the rhymes come from and what was their intent than what we may gain from them by considering them in the way here presented.

In the final analysis, and after the demands of scholarly accuracy are met, the truth or falsity of any theory is ultimately subject to confirmation or rejection by the reader at a purely intuitive and experiential level. Furthermore, we tend to learn for the most part only what we know, and cannot learn what we do not know. That is to say, when the familiar spark of recognition is lit within us by a word, a phrase, or an idea, no amount of logical argument is likely to dissuade us from its truth. Our minds may be persuaded by such argument, but we will never be convinced at the deeper inner level where we live.

And it is to that deeper level within each of us that both the *Tao Teh Ching* and these rhymes seem to be addressed. For that reason this book is dedicated to those who may have been predisposed by their interests and experience to understand and accept it.

Acknowledgements

The author wishes to thank Princeton University Press for permission to reproduce works from their publications (pps. 77, 89, 136); Checkerboard Press, a division of Macmillan Publishing, for permission to reproduce illustrations by Blanche Fisher Wright (pps. 36, 117); Budek Films and Slides, for permission to reproduce the Josetsu painting (p. 162); St. Andrews College, for permission to reproduce slides and prints from their collection; and Mr. Bill Stoffel, for his assistance.

I
The Tao

Symbol of the Tao, ink painting by the author

THE BEGINNING: A Preface to God and Man

> And the earth was without form, and void;
> and darkness was upon the face of the deep.
> And the Spirit of God moved upon the face
> of the waters.[1]

Whether it is the Hebrew story from the book of Genesis, an Egyptian, Chinese, or North American Indian story, the essential story of creation remains very much the same wherever it is told: There is first an airy or watery darkness, or a void:

> The Tao is a void,
> Used but never filled:
> An abyss it is,
> Like an ancestor
> From which all things come.[2]

And in this Primal Chaos, there resides a spirit, a power, or a mystery:

> Something there is, whose veiled creation was
> Before the earth or sky began to be;
> So silent, so aloof and so alone,
> It changes not, nor fails, but touches all:
> Conceive it as the mother of the world.[3]

We may call it "mother of the world," "Spirit of God," the Godhead, or the Tao. It has been given many names. But it is the

Source and the Origin of all things. It is the Supreme Principle which initiates, inspires, flows through, and regulates the cosmos. It is the Beginning from which all being comes. In the words of the *Tao Teh Ching:*

> A deep pool it is, never to run dry!
> Whose offspring it may be I do not know:
> It is like a preface to God.[4]

This Beginning, this Oneness, may be further described as the Formless which precedes all forms, the Soundless which inspires all sounds, the Nameless which pervades all names; it is the Non-Being which precedes all being. From this Imperishable Unity arises our world of perishable multiplicity; from this Infinite and Eternal is created the finite and the temporal.

The particulars of how this is accomplished may vary from one creation story to the next, but in each the furnishing of the world takes place in twos—the Oneness gives rise to the Two and the world of dualities is born.

In Genesis, creation proceeds in pairs of opposites: light is first divided from darkness, then heaven from earth; sea and land are separated, and the sun is created to rule the day, the moon to rule the night. Plants are created in two kinds—those that bear their seed within and those that bear it without. Creatures for the skies and creatures for the seas appear; then creatures for the land, in two kinds, those that walk and those that creep upon its surface. And lastly comes another pair: man, created from the dust of the earth, and woman.

In Taoist thought as well, the One begets the Two: and here the two are called Yin and Yang. They are the fundamental male and female principles, the regulators of the seasons, complementary and mutually necessary opposites, which govern all the changeable world. Yin, the feminine principle, is darkness, cold, wetness, softness, passivity, and such. Yang, the male principle, is light, warmth, dryness, hardness, activity, and the like. It is through the interaction of these two primary principles that all the changing phenomena of our world are produced.

In the traditions of both East and West, the Oneness gives rise to the Two, and the story of human life on the planet begins. And however these stories of creation may be understood—as superstition, myth, divine revelation, or historical fact—it is important to consider that modern biological theories of organic evolution and the investigation of DNA and contemporary cosmogonies that describe an expanding universe do nothing to contradict their common basic theme: *that of an initial unity from which arises multiplicity.*

However grand the Two may be, it is a lessening, a division, and a diminution of the

One. And as life forms continue to flourish and develop in their diversity, this lessening, this sense of diminution, gives rise in us to a longing for the One, a nostalgia for the paradise of our origins. There is born in us a sense of alienation, a feeling of being irretrievably cut off from the Source. This separation is described in the biblical story of The Fall.

Along with this sense of separation from the Oneness, there is born the need for religion. Taken from the Latin prefix *re* meaning "back," and the verb *ligare* meaning "to bind," religion is a binding back together of that which has become divided. In fact the primary motivation in every religion has been to bind us back together with the One, to regain and re-establish on whatever literal or symbolic level the Oneness from which we sense we are derived.

Whatever else has motivated humanity, this powerful longing has been our greatest need. From their earliest development, our social and governmental systems, our arts and architecture and sciences—all of our earthly systems of order—were arranged as microcosmic and mesocosmic reflections of the "heavenly order" apparent in the workings of nature. The earliest *constructed* housing seems to have been domical, a microcosmic echo of the 'heavenly dome' of the skies above. (Our words domicile and domestic still reveal their origins in the Latin and Greek words for house, *domus* and *doma.*)

Early city plans and calendars alike were arranged in a cyclic fashion, reflecting the circular earthly plane and the cycle of time, and each was divided into four parts, in imitation of the four directions and the four seasons. Kings were equated with the sun, ruler of the heavens; queens were associated with the moon and the Earth. Even the names for the days of the week were originally derived from the sun, the moon, and the five visible planets. In fact most early human effort in every sphere of activity not directed solely at physical survival can be demonstrated to have been influenced strongly and directly by this basic need for "re-ligion," for binding us back together with the Oneness.

In this sense, religion can be said to exist for the irreligious, for those who are not "bound back." For where there is no sense of alienation, no feeling of separateness, there can be no need for religion. The history of the world's religions may be described most simply then as the Two yearning for the One, as the world of man and multiplicity longing for the Heaven of God and Unity.

The best-known Christian prayer seeks this union of the heavenly and earthly Two with a powerful plea to its God:

7

Thy Will be done on earth as it is in
Heaven.

But the plea, in a sense, contains its own
negation. The statement ''Thy'' will (unless
understood in the special sense Martin Buber
describes in his *I and Thou)* is a positive
recognition and an assertion of separateness,
of duality and division. It infers a world of
Self and Other, of God and man, of I and It.
And this state, confirmed in the words of the
prayer, is the very thing the prayer seeks to
overcome.

It is as though, suddenly aware of the
separateness of our two hands, we desperately
wish to merge them into one. Obviously the
only way this can occur is when there is no
desire and the two hands are joined and absorbed in a common task. And this is most
clearly symbolized in the joining of the two
hands, which is common in both Christian
and Oriental traditions, in attitudes of prayer
and meditation.

In the Christian practice, the hands are
joined, palms together, and placed at the
level of the heart or the head, where they are
aimed together upward and outward, *away*
from the self. In this way, the whole being of
the worshipper is symbolically brought together and focused at the location thought to
be its center (the heart or the head), then

aimed or projected toward a greater Being *without.*

In Oriental traditions of meditation, the hands usually point *toward* one another and are cupped, palms upward; the thumbs are brought lightly together at their tips to form a flattened circle between the palms and the thumbs. The hands, joined in this way, are then held in the lap next to the lower abdomen. In this way, the whole being of the meditator is symbolically brought together and concentrated at the spot thought to be its center (in this case, the belly, or the *hara*),* and focused on the greater Being within.

The simple and profound differences between the two practices illustrate quite clearly the fundamental contrasts and similarities between the two traditions. Each demands an intense centering and focusing of the spiritual energy of the worshiper. But the way of the West is linear; once focused, the energy and concentration are directed in a line away from the self and outward to a God above.

---

*The negative side of these two examples is contained in Western and traditional Japanese approaches to suicide. Taken by the desire to destroy the very center and essence of his "self," the Westener is likely to aim a gun at his head or heart, while the Japanese practice traditionally used a blade to commit *harakiri* (a "belly cut").

9

Oriental traditions form a self-contained circle with the hands, and the circle is centered on the lower belly, thus focusing the meditative energy downward and inward to a God within.

In either practice when desire of any kind is present, there can be no successful communion with God. In order for desire to exist, there must be a duality of subject and object. Desire is synonymous with awareness of separateness from the thing desired; desire and duality are coexistent.

How we have attempted to hear the sound of "one hand clapping," how we have sought to effect our binding back together with the One, is a story written in the history of art, science, and religions, with their doctrines, dogma, rituals, beliefs, teachings, and practices. It is the one most fundamental and fascinating story of all.

However else we may respond to the stories of creation, we should recognize that the process they describe exists every bit as much in the present moment and in the future as in past. If these stories describe our collective beginning, they describe our individual origins as well. For the process of creation is one that is daily and constantly repeated, renewed, and re-experienced by us all. Consider the way life is conceived and brought into our world: the two—male and female—are joined and "reunited," and where there was nothing, something is miraculously begun. The prenatal infant floats in the darkness of the amniotic waters, bound together with and within its source in the mother. And when the infant is born— emerges and is divided from that source—it encounters the world of dualities in much the same order as they are described in Genesis.

First the baby is exposed to light, where before there was only darkness, and to air and dryness and cold, where there was only watery wetness and warmth. The baby encounters form and space, where before they were undifferentiated, and all space was filled. He learns of man and woman, of creatures great and small. And as he grows, and when he is an adult, he will continue to participate in the creation story, as a million new cells are daily born within him.

The Beginning: An End to God and Man

For man, both collectively and individually, the desire to return to the womb of his origins—in the broadest and deepest sense—the desire to be bound back together with the Source, is perhaps the most persistent, deeply

11

rooted, and intense desire of all. It is the very basis for the religious instinct, the motivation which lies at the base of every religion, and is manifest in countless ways both secular and spiritual. But if it is the highest and most noble human goal, it is also the source of our deepest frustration.

By their very nature, attempts to institutionalize the Tao—to make known the Unknown, to define the Indefinable—are in many ways self-defeating. These fixative efforts, recorded in the history of organized religions, may be likened to the story of Chaos, as told by Chuang-tze, the third century B.C. Chinese philosopher. In the story, Chaos (or what we have called the Oneness, the Godhead, the Tao) is the cause of the achievements of his followers. They recognize that this is so, and wish to repay him. Seeing that Chaos has no sense organs by which to discriminate, they resolve to help him, and do so by first giving him eyes, another day a nose, and so on, until in the space of a week they have transformed him into a creature like themselves. And, as D. T. Suzuki reported in a splendid essay, "while they were congratulating themselves on their success, Chaos died."[5]

This is nothing less than the death of God *through the well-meaning efforts of his followers!* Friedrich Nietzsche, a Western philosopher with a similar understanding, wrote in 1882,

"God is dead. God remains dead. And we have killed him."[6] Nietzsche—who has often and mistakenly been understood as anti-Christ when he was merely anti-Christian—felt not only that Christians had killed their God, but that they had come to worship the very antithesis of everything He stood for:

> Mankind lies on its knees before the opposite of that which was the origin, the meaning, the *right* of the evangel; in the concept of 'church' it has pronounced holy precisely what the 'bringer of glad tidings' felt to be *beneath* and *behind* himself—one would look in vain for a greater example of world historical irony.[7]

Put in the terms used by medieval churchman Meister Eckhardt, "to seek God by rituals is to get the ritual and lose God in the process, for He hides behind it."[8] Or, in the words of the *Tao Teh Ching:*

> The secret waits for the insight
> Of eyes unclouded by longing;
> Those who are bound by desire
> See only the outward container.[9]

The meaning of these authors is clear: Chaos, Godhead, or Tao, the Primal Unity, the Oneness, the Beginning, the Infinite and Ineffable "secret" behind all of life—call it what we will—is unfathomable, unnameable,

13

ungraspable. When we seek to make it finite, to divide it into parts, to fathom and to chart its depths, we cannot but fail. For stilled waters must surely become stagnant.

This tendency for the fixed and known to become a stagnant, corrupt, and isolated pool, only dimly reminiscent of the great Sea of the Unknown from which it was born, may have been a familiar idea to three of our greatest teachers: Buddha, Socrates, and Christ. For none of the three committed his teachings to the fixed and written word, none created any system, structure, or organizational hierarchy to promulgate his teachings. With each, the teaching was carried out orally and person-to-person, and in the living moment of the present.

Here is a great paradox: obviously we will not seek for God, will not search for the "secret," unless we desire it, and desire it greatly. Yet we are told, "those who are bound by desire see only the outward container." But if the invisible cannot be brought into the visible world, if the Infinite cannot be made finite, how then may it ever be approached at all? If we are doomed by our very desire to see only the outward container, how may we ever know the secret? The *Tao Teh Ching* answers:

> These two come paired but distinct
> By their names.

14

Of all things profound,
Say that their pairing is deepest,
The gate to the root of the world.[10]

It is a cryptic answer, but that is the only
kind of answer we are likely to get.

The texts of the world's religious teachings,
particularly the traditions of mysticism, in
both the East and West, offer the seeker instruction in approaching the unapproachable.
They all seem to share a passion for the cryptic and paradoxical response, a tendency to
speak in terms which defy our rational attempts to understand them. For theirs is a
tradition that lives and is transmitted *outside
the fixed world of Time and History, beyond the
realm of logic and words and the rationality of waking consciousness.*

On the surface, their pronouncements are
often frustratingly illogical, baffling, and absurd, sometimes to the point of seeming silly.
In fact, this is a part of their aim: to lure us
on beyond the boundaries of the sensible
world, beyond the fixed, known, material,
and conscious plane, and into the timeless sea
of the unconscious wherein dwells the Tao.

The journey, if we attempt it, is most difficult and fraught with powerful dangers,
which are no less real for the fact that they
are hidden from normal view. This journey is
described symbolically over and again in
myth and dream and fable, as Joseph

15

Campbell eloquently points out in his account, *The Hero with a Thousand Faces*.[11] Each such journey requires letting go, relinquishing our grip on the safe and familiar haven of the known, and plunging headlong into the abyss, the wilderness, or the sea of the unconscious. There we encounter adventures and horrors unimagined before we may find the Tao:

By letting go, it all gets done;
The world is won by those who let it go![12]

Paradoxically, this noble and life-affirming search must end, if it is to be successful, in our own extinction. Eastern and Western traditions alike insist that the death of the individual and personal self, the negation of the separate ego, is required before the greater reality, the ''secret,'' may be found. In words reported by Matthew to be those of Christ: ''He that loseth his life for my sake shall find it.''[13] And in the *Tao Teh Ching,* ''The Wise Man chooses to be last and so becomes the first of all; denying self, he too is saved''[14]; or, in another passage, ''Then, though you die, you shall not perish.''[15]

This selfless state of perfection, if reached, also means the end of all desire, the end of preferences, attachment, and differentiation, as Christ described in his injunction to be perfect, even as God is perfect: "for he maketh his sun to rise on the evil and on the good, and sendeth rain on the just and on the unjust."[16]

Even more alarming perhaps is that this enlightenment and awakening means, in a sense, the death of God. For when the One is re-created, when Unity is attained, there can no longer be the separate duality of God and Man. Their duality has been transcended. For one who is "bound back together," God and religion are as unnecessary, unnatural, and irrelevant as lungs for a fish.

For the rest of us, however, some swimming lessons may be required before we enter the great sea of the unconscious. These lessons are available in the cryptic literature of mystical teachings in many cultures, and they are not so different from one another as we might suppose. Perhaps the simplest possible condensation of the many teachings is contained in the following statement:

Not Two and Not One

What this means, briefly, is that the fundamental secret of Heaven and earth, of God and man, is that *they are not separate and yet not the same.* The secret and the outward container "come paired but distinct by their names"—like the symbol for Yin-Yang:

Each half of the basic duality contains the seed of its opposite, and both are bound together in a whole. They *are* separate, they are a duality, yet they are also not separate, they are one. They are the same and inseparable One, yet they are also not the same, for the world of duality does exist. Whether we refer to the two halves as Yin and Yang, God and man, or the Infinite and the finite, each lives within the other; they are not separate and not the same, Not Two and Not One.

To master this idea intellectually is not too difficult. The idea that the Infinite and finite are closely bound together is not even an unfamiliar notion; a number of writers and thinkers have suggested as much. Tennyson, in his poem about the flower in the crannied wall, realized that the small flower might contain the secret:

> Little flower - but if I could understand
> What you are, root and all, and all in all, I
> should know what God and man is.[17]*

---

*For a brilliant discussion of Tennyson's poem, how it represents the Western way of knowing, and contrasts

Tennyson seems to have gained a fleeting glimpse of the Infinite, at least enough to know it is there. And that is not so difficult. One can learn to leap up far enough to glimpse the sublime, and may even do so repeatedly, each time falling back (as one must) into the finite existence which we all share. Having done so, one then becomes, in Kierkegaard's phrase, a "knight of infinite resignation,"[18] reconciled to the irreversible and complete division between the Infinite world of the One, which was glimpsed, and the finite world of dualities, in which we live.

Those who leap up in this way gain a certain nobility of spirit in this exercise, and stand out from the multitudes who are confined solely to finite, worldly joys and sorrows. They know the meaning of the teaching "not two and not one," and have glimpsed the One, but still *live* in the world of the two.

Greater by far is Kierkegaard's "knight of faith," a rare and enlightened aristocrat of the spirit who has also glimpsed Infinity, but who has passed beyond the state of resignation to its utter inaccessibility, and has somehow magically learned to *live* the Infinite within the very heart of the finiteness which contains us all. These enlightened ones have learned that "if you cannot find the justification of existence in an act as simple as that of

---

to the Eastern, see D. T. Suzuki's essay in *Zen Buddhism and Psychoanalysis.*

19

doing the dishes, you will find it nowhere."[19]
They have learned to live simultaneously in
the world of the One and the world of the
Two—and they are *not* separate! And they
are *not* the same!

II
The Mother

Venus of Willendorf, c. 16,000-10,000 B.C.,
Museum of Natural History, Vienna

The Mother of Songs, the mother of our
whole seed, bore us in the beginning. She is
the mother of all races of men and the
mother of all tribes. She is the mother of the
thunder, the mother of the rivers, the
mother of trees and of all kinds of things.
She is the mother of songs and dances. She
is the mother of the older brother stones.
She is the mother of the grain and the
mother of all things. . . . She is the mother of
the animals, the only one, and the mother of
the Milky Way. . . . She alone is the mother
of things, she alone. . . [1]

*W*HEN THE Oneness which we seek is referred to in the world's myth and religion,
folk tale and fable, it is described in almost as
many ways and tongues as there have been
attempts to describe it. But most often it is
found personified in figures, such as the
deities who have peopled the world's faiths of
the past and present. And these superhuman
entities have served as the objects of our
greatest love, devotion, and longing, our most
intense envy, fear, and loathing, since we
first began to leave any record of our existence on the planet.

Some of the earliest references to such beings as these are contained in the carvings,
drawings, and incised images of preliterate
man (see illustration). And even here the dual
nature of the Oneness is found expressed in

archetypal images of both male and female figures.

Perhaps it is understandable that early man should have equated his collective origins with the sources of individual life, and made of his earthly parents models for a "heavenly two," who initiated all of creation. Whether or not the explanation for the pair of prototypes is that simple is something we can never truly know.

We may, however, acknowledge that there is a basic male-female dualism encountered almost uniformly in the earliest myths and religions in cultures throughout the world. In these, it is the female principle that is most commonly associated with the forces of the earth, and the male principle that serves to represent the forces of the sky or the heavens. Thus we have the twin ideas of a "heavenly father" and an "earthly mother," which are still preserved in modern religious belief.

The earth becomes the Mother of us all. We are born from her, as in the Old Testament, when God, the "Heavenly Father," molds the first man from the dust of the earth. And when we die, we return to her; this return is celebrated in both, real and a symbolic fashion in the myriad of burial customs in which the bodies of the dead are literally placed into the earth, thereby returning them to the womb of the Great Mother.

In some cultures, the female aspect has

been regarded as the more powerful of the two; in others the male commanded the greatest devotion and respect. It should be stressed, however, that the diversities and contradictions contained within each of the two and the complexities of their interrelationship defy any simple explanation. Certainly we should not attempt to understand or to dismiss them too quickly.

In the very broadest sense, each of the thousands of gods and goddesses of the world's faiths may be explained simply as a lesser or a greater manifestation of the Great Mother or the Great Father. Each god and goddess in the Greek Pantheon, for example, may be described as embodying and controlling certain aspects and functions of one or the other of the two.

In the trinities—which are known both in Christianity (the Father, the Son, the Holy Spirit) and in Hinduism (Brahma, the Creator; Vishnu, the Preserver; Shiva, the Destroyer)—we might perceive a tripartite manifestation of the Great Father. But such explanations are simplistic and at least partially incorrect.

While it is true, in a sense, that each of these masculine trinities is but a subdivision of the Great Father, it is also true, in a much larger sense, that each is a manifestation of the Oneness, and includes *both* male and female principles. For each of the trinities

25

controls both the creative and destructive functions; each contains both the positive and the negative aspects governing life and death.

In a corresponding sense the *Tao Teh Ching* refers to the "mother of the world," using the feminine principle as an all-embracing symbol for the whole:

> The valley spirit is not dead:
> They say it is the mystic female.
> Her gateway is, they further say,
> The base of earth and heaven.[2]

Here it is the female principle which combines earth and heaven and serves as the embodiment of the One.

In fact, the archetypes of the Great Mother and the Great Father, as they appear in myth and religion, are both extremely fluid and mercurial, and it is quite often impossible to clearly differentiate one from the other.

Like Yin and Yang, when taken together they constitute the All, the Oneness, the hermaphroditic Godhead. Yet each contains the seed of the other, and thus, when taken separately, each contains both positive and negative aspects, and each may be seen as containing the Oneness within itself. This is an idea that we will re-examine, in a slightly different and more personal context.

The earth as Mother, as the Great Goddess, in world myth is met in literally hun-

dreds of guises and under countless names
and titles. She is Isis, Nut, and Maat,
Gorgon and Sophia; she is Kali, Shakti,
Tara, and Kwan-Yin; she is Demeter, Kore,
and Aphrodite. When Christianity appeared,
most of her local faces and functions in the
Mediterranean area were absorbed into the
figure of Mary, the Madonna, Mother of
Christ.

Erich Neumann thoroughly discusses and
describes this primordial Feminine Principle
her many names and aspects, and their
meaning, in his book *The Great Mother*.[3] He
traces not only the positive characteristics of
the Goddess, but what he calls her "negative
elementary character" as well. For nature is
as often cruel as benevolent. She may create,
sustain, and nourish us, but she is also the
Terrible Mother, the Devouring Mother, who
kills us all.

If the Great Mother has been represented
in a bewildering diversity of forms and functions, it should be acknowledged that the
Great Father has, as well. Like the Great
Mother, he too has been known for both his
creative and destructive powers, has been
both benevolent and cruel, both adored and
feared.

It is important to recognize that, like the
creation story, these archetypal and cosmic

male and female principles have counterparts and corresponding equivalents, which are found expressed in each of our individual psyches and our individual lives.

To understand how this may be so, we will borrow Carl Jung's terms *anima* and *animus* to designate the Great Mother and the Great Father, respectively, as they are manifest in the unconscious mind of the individual.

The anima refers to the shadowy and mysterious feminine presence which most males encounter, at one time or another in their lives, in dreams. She may appear in forms that are youthful, mischievous, and capricious—as a siren, a nymphet, a "Lolita"; she may appear older and more knowing, as a witch, a sorceress, a gypsy, a negress; she may appear in any combination of these and other forms, as a wife, a mother, a sister, and she may quickly change her character from one to another of these during the course of a single dream. She may be the girl next door and the Queen of Heaven; she may be beautiful or beastly or both, alluring and desirable and terrifying as well. She is both Life and Death.

The animus is the corresponding masculine personification of the male principle that resides in the unconscious of the female. In her dreams, he may appear as a brother, a father, a son; as a priest, a lover, a rapist, a sorcerer, a pirate, or a magician, and in other forms, as well as in any combination of such forms; he may be at once horrifying and irresistibly attractive.

Most of us will recall encountering such figures in our dreams. In Jung's words, "in the unconscious of every man there is hidden a feminine personality, and in that of every woman a masculine personality."[4] In other words, the basic Oneness, expressed in the male-female duality of the Great Mother and the Great Father, also lives complete within each of us. Buried beneath male consciousness lies a feminine complement, and beneath female consciousness, a masculine counterpart.

Traditionally, maleness, like Yang, has been equated with the "light" of rationality, logic, order, and activity; and femaleness, like Yin, has been accepted as embodying the "darker" elements of irrationality, intuition, creativity, and passivity. So it seems understandable that when we seek a mate, a "better half" as folk wisdom expresses it, we are symbolically seeking our own integration, wholeness, and perfection. We are seeking to "marry" the surface and the hidden halves of ourselves, most often by finding a mate who outwardly personifies and embodies the very qualities which, in ourselves, are most deeply buried.

This process of projection should be fairly clear to most of us—if not in ourselves, and our own choices of partners, then in the selections of some of those we know. For we are all acquainted with the excessively masculine or "macho" type of male, who marries a correspondingly excessively submissive and gentle female; and with the opposite example of the more creative, sensitive, passive, gentle, or otherwise "feminine" male who marries an efficient, orderly, logical, or otherwise aggressive and "masculine" woman. These are extreme and simplistic examples, to be sure. The male and female who are themselves less extreme in their conscious maleness and femaleness would tend to seek partners who are also less extreme.

Obviously the process of selecting a mate is a complex one, with many factors involved beyond those outlined here. But this principle of projection and compensation is an important one and perfectly normal. It forces us into the recognition that, in a very real sense, even the way in which we choose our mates is a symbolic reflection of the urge toward integration, the desire for Oneness. If the creation story is continually repeated in a microcosmic fashion in the birth and development of each individual, then the union of the Great Mother and the Great Father is daily played out, symbolically, in religious and civil ceremonies, in churches and temples and justice-of-the-peace offices throughout the land.

The Mother—Sublime and Ridiculous

What we have been discussing on a number of levels, and in a number of ways, is the *coincidence of opposites,* which is represented in the symbol for Yin-Yang, and which combines:

both the One and the Two,
both the Infinite and the Finite,
both the Heavenly Father and the Earthly
    Mother,
both that which is within and that which is
    without.

The Yin-Yang symbol very neatly binds up *all* of life's polarities, representing both their fundamental opposition and their complementarity. And, as we have seen, the coincidence of opposites may be found expressed in the psychology of the individual, in the anima and the animus, as well as on a more mythical and universal level. But, as we have also seen, it is not limited to the macrocosmic and the microcosmic levels of the universal and the individual. It appears just as clearly ex-

31

pressed at the mesocosmic level, in the early development of humanity's social or collective being, in architecture, arts, and sciences, as well as in myth and religion. And it appears in more modern periods of history as well.

In modern physics, the coincidence of opposites is known as the principle of complementarity. In biology, Nobel laureate Jacques Monod describes as the "central problem of biology" the "profound epistemological contradiction" between nature's "objectivity" and the "teleonomic character of living organisms."[5] In other words, the "cornerstone of the scientific method," the assumption that nature is objective, that it cannot be understood as working toward any purpose, seems to be flatly contradicted by the fact that living organisms *do* have a teleonomic character, that "in their structure and performance they act projectively—realize and pursue a purpose."

"Purposeless purpose"—a contradiction in terms, a coincidence of opposites—is well known in the *Tao Teh Ching,* where it is called *wu wei,* creative quietude or actionless action. In modern literature, we find similar examples of the coincidence of opposites, as in the figure of the wise man or the sage, which is frequently interchangeable with that of the fool, madman, idiot, or clown. Dostoevsky tapped at the very roots of spirituality and created a character closely akin to a savior, in his portrait of *The Idiot*.[6] Nietzsche chose the character of a madman, just as Shakespeare used a clown, to deliver some of his most profound (and puzzling) observations.

Similarly, some of the most penetrating and complex truths contained in the world's religious literature are expressed in the simplest and briefest forms, as aphorisms, parables, proverbs, or in an Eastern tradition, as mondos and koans. Taoism and Zen Buddhism, particularly, tend to express the sublime in the form of the cryptic statement, sometimes maddeningly simple to the point of absurdity, so that it sounds nonsensical and ridiculous.

Indeed, our greatest writers and thinkers seem to have understood that the tragic and the comic are truly not separate and not the same; that, as the Sioux medicine man Black Elk expressed it, "the truth comes into this world with two faces. One is sad with suffering, and the other laughs; but it is the same face, laughing or weeping."[7] Such men of genius seem to know that it is not uncommon for the extremes of lunacy and lucidity to coincide. Even the word we use to describe such thinkers, "genius," carries not only the familiar connotation of extreme intellectual ability, but literally means that the person described is inhabited by a *jinni,* or demoniacal spirit.

Truthfully, even in our most routine and

mundane emotions and affairs, opposites are often more closely interwoven and interdependent than we commonly dare to perceive. Sense and nonsense are not so very far apart, after all, and tend to collide and intermix at their extremes.

So perhaps it will not be too outrageous to suggest that the sublime figure of the Great Mother may have her lesser, more ridiculous manifestations as well. The familiar and slightly absurd figure of Mother Goose may be one of these. This mythical old lady, who rides through the air on a goose, a teller of tales, riddles, and nonsense rhymes meant for children—can she be a lesser incarnation, a folk version, of the Great Goddess herself?

III
Mother Goose

Mother Goose, from The Real Mother Goose, *by Blanche Fisher Wright*

A LARGE PART of the work of Carl Jung was directed at identifying and investigating what he chose to call the "collective unconscious." While there can be no brief and truly adequate definition for the term, the collective unconscious may be described as an inborn and hidden repository of timeless motifs, images, associations, and meanings— "a psychic system of a collective, universal and impersonal nature which is identical in all individuals."[1] He distinguishes this collective unconscious from both the personal, individual consciousness and the *personal* unconscious. It differs from the latter in that its contents are archetypal and "owe their existence exclusively to heredity."[2]

Within the collective unconscious, according to Jung, there exists a whole range of archetypal images, such as the Great Mother and the Great Father, already discussed. These primordial images are projected and expressed through both our collective mythology and our individual dreams. A basic motif such as the Great Mother will emerge in the myth of a given culture in a form appropriate to the consciousness of that culture, and will similarly emerge in the dream of an individual with some of its coloration and characteristics furnished by the personal unconscious of the dreamer. In other words, these archetypal images, which live unchanged in the collective unconscious, are universal motifs that may take on different outward manifestations appropriate to the culture in whose myth they appear; though timeless and unchanging, they may assume slightly different aspects appropriate to the personal unconscious of the dreamer in whose dreams they emerge.

Jung was able to posit the existence of this collective unconscious in a completely convincing and persuasive fashion, and amassed an enormous amount of evidence, from myth and dream alike, which "proved" his thesis as thoroughly as any such thesis as this is ever likely to be proven. He demonstrated, for example, that in the dream sequences of his patients, the dreamer frequently encountered signs, symbols, and very specific images with which the dreamer had no previous conscious familarity whatever. Yet these were duplicated, with amazing fidelity and detail, not only in the dreams of others, but in the signs, symbols, and images of traditional art and myth in many widely divergent cultures.

The truly incredible extent to which these dreams duplicated and paralleled their more ancient and esoteric mythical counterparts is a fascinating study. One must read Jung's works fully to appreciate the connections between myth and dream.

We may return to the subject, but for the moment, perhaps we may accept the possibility that fundamental archetypes such as the

Great Mother do exist, and that they appear in the myths of widely separated cultures. Further, the Great Mother, along with other archetypes, may appear in superficially different forms, each appropriate for the particular culture in which it appears.

Next we must consider that the post-Renaissance period in the development of Western cultures—which produced the figure of Mother Goose—has tended overwhelmingly to favor the growth of rational, physical, and material concerns over the deeper unconscious and spiritual drives that animated and inspired the myth and religion of earlier periods in history. With the rise of scientific and pragmatic materialism, there has been a corresponding decline in the centrality and importance of myth and religion.

In the present era, then, it seems understandable that if the Great Mother is to be found preserved at all, it will be in a relatively despiritualized and somewhat innocuous form, or at least in a less awesome manifestation than those which peopled the myth of earlier cultures. She will be the Hollywood sex goddess, for example, rather than Aphrodite or the Madonna.

In an age given over to fascination with computer technology and televised sports, it seems entirely appropriate that the archetypal Feminine Principle should also be reduced in the mythology of childhood to an absurd old lady who tells nonsense meant for children. The personification of the Great Goddess as Mother Goose represents another collision of the sublime and the ridiculous, the wise and the foolish. It is another coincidence of opposites, and not an unworthy one. Every culture has had its share of popular clowns and fools, tricksters, witches, and "old storytellers." Mother Goose, with her collection of tales, riddles, and rhymes, is certainly not less well known, not less foolish, and not less wise than any of them, as we shall presently begin to discover.

The actual historical origins of the character Mother Goose are thoroughly researched and thoroughly unclear. She has been known to us at least since the sixteenth or seventeenth century, and may well have been known much earlier. She has been identified by scholars as deriving from various specific historical personalities, including Queen Bertha, mother of Charlemagne, who died in 783 A.D., and another Bertha, wife of Robert II of France (c. 970-1031 A.D.), both of whom seem to have had embarrassingly large feet: they were known, respectively, as "Queen Goose-foot" and "Goose-footed Bertha." Some American scholars jealously identify Mother Goose instead with a lady of Boston, stepmother to ten children and

mother to six others who bore the surname
Goose; her son-in-law published a volume of
Mother Goose melodies in 1719. Some
scholars, presumably serious, have even iden-
tified Mother Goose with the Queen of
Sheba.

Without challenging the truth of any of
these associations, it is nonetheless fair to
suggest that the mythical importance and
psychological validity and necessity for such a
figure as teller of tales for children is far better established in the writings of Jung, Neumann, and others of a similar persuasion.

The image of Mother Goose as a benevolent and wise old story-teller is undeniably
paralleled in world myth in numerous and
various manifestations of the Great Mother
figures. The demonic or malevolent aspects of
the Great Goddess, as reflected in such
manifestations as the Hindu goddess Kali, are
not entirely unknown to our friendly Mother
Goose either. In fact, most of the earliest illustrations of Mother Goose depict her as a
witch-like figure, strongly reminiscent of some
of the shadowy forms of the anima, described
by Jung in his analyses of dreams. This
aspect of the Mother carries not only the
fruitful, regenerative, and benevolent qualities
of Mother Nature, but also her capacity for
storm and strife.

Mother Goose may easily be seen as embodying these darker elements of the anima,

particularly if we consider the complete collection of rhymes which are associated with her. For many of the rhymes are ribald, tragic, and threatening, even violent. One writer, urging nursery rhyme reform as recently as 1952, claimed that in a survey of 200 traditional Mother Goose rhymes, 100 "harbour unsavoury elements."³ He went on to cite a list of these, which included:

8 allusions to murder (unclassified),
2 cases of choking to death,
1 case of death by devouring,
1 case of cutting a human being in half,
1 case of decapitation,
1 case of death by squeezing,
1 case of death by shrivelling,
1 case of death by starvation,
1 case of boiling to death,
1 case of death by hanging,
1 case of death by drowning,
4 cases of killing domestic animals,
1 case of body snatching,
21 cases of death (unclassified),
7 cases relating to the severing of limbs,
1 case of the desire to have a limb severed,
2 cases of self-inflicted injury,
4 cases relating to the breaking of limbs,
1 allusion to a bleeding heart,
1 case of devouring human flesh,
5 threats of death,
1 case of kidnapping,
12 cases of torment and cruelty to human beings and animals,
8 cases of whipping and lashing,
3 allusions to blood,

14 cases of stealing and general dishonesty,
15 allusions to maimed human beings and
  animals,
1 allusion to undertakers,
2 allusions to graves,
23 cases of physical violence (unclassified),
1 case of lunacy,
16 allusions to misery and sorrow,
1 case of drunkenness,
4 cases of cursing,
1 allusion to marriage as a form of death,
1 case of scorning the blind,
1 case of scorning prayer,
9 cases of children being lost or abandoned,
2 cases of house burning,
9 allusions to poverty and want,
5 allusions to quarreling,
2 cases of unlawful imprisonment,
2 cases of racial discrimination.[4]

Let it suffice to say, then, that Mother Goose does indeed have a darker side.

This alone is not enough to qualify her as an incarnation of the Great Goddess, Mother Nature. But what of her name and her association with a goose? Certainly the name, as teller of tales, rather than author of rhymes, goes back at least to 1650.[5] Can we trust the nursery rhyme scholars' explanation that she derives from a specific lady with unfortunately large and goose-like feet, who lived 1000 years ago? Or from a lady with the surname Goose, who lived in Boston in the seventeenth century? Neither explanation even begins to justify the continued accept-

Wild Goose, ink painting by Mu Ch'i, 13th century China, Berlin Ostasiatisches Museum

ance and appropriateness, for hundreds of years, of an old lady, associated somehow with a goose, as teller of tales and rhymes for children. In order to appreciate any deeper mythical and psychological validity and meaning in the figure of Mother Goose, it is helpful to know something of the goose itself, and its traditional mythical and symbolic associations.

The Goose

Being associated with the earth and its life forms, the Great Mother has been presented variously as embodied in or associated with a number of different plants and animals, intimately at first, and later in a more distant fashion. Thus she frequently appears in early myth and art as either wholly or partly in the actual form of some creature, such as a goose, a lioness, or a snake. "Later though she ceases to *be* the goose itself but rides on it or wears its symbol on her cloak; and she ceases to *be* the lioness, but stands on it. She no longer *is* the serpent but is accompanied by it. At this later stage, she becomes a goddess in human form, ruling over the animal kingdom."[6] It is in this way that she becomes the symbolic "ruler over the unconscious powers that still take on animal form in our dreams."[7]

45

This identification of the godly with the beastly, known as theriomorphism, is as common in world myth for the Great Father as for the Great Mother (consider Zeus and his myriad forms). And the basis for such associations seems clear. Throughout human history certain plants, animals, birds, fishes, and even insects have been held in special awe and esteem for their particularly impressive characteristics of behavior, appearance, or real or imagined abilities. These were among the very earliest subjects to be represented in the history of the visual arts.

Birds have always held an understandable fascination, since the wonder and appeal of flight is commonly felt and shared by us all. The freedom from the earthbound, which it symbolizes, has played an important role in our myths and dreams alike, and the bird has become the most common emblem of transcendence. The symbolic idea of flight as a necessity for penetrating beyond the confines of the finite world is a familiar one, shared and expressed equally in figures as dissimilar as Peter Pan and the dove of the Holy Spirit. Allegorical references to birds and their flight are commonly met in the myth and literature of every culture.

Among the birds that have appeared most frequently as symbols are the eagle, hawk, raven, vulture, dove, owl, stork, and goose. Universally these have enjoyed a greater mythical importance than, for example, the sparrow, and it is not difficult to understand why.

The goose is impressive for its sheer size and shape, the grace and purposefulness of its flight in great flocks, the regularity of its migrations north and south, the poignance of its cry heard in the distance from an autumn sky, and for its legendary faithfulness to its mate. It is a swamp bird as well, as it moves in three elements: earth, air, and water. This association lends the goose a mystery it might not have if it preferred the plain or prairie. None of these things went unnoticed or unappreciated in earlier cultures, when people lived in more intimate contact with the natural world.

In pagan Sweden, the goose was used as a grave offering, and in Germany it was sacrificed to Odin, god of magic, ecstasy, and the dead, at the time of the autumnal equinox. Early travelers to Siberia "noted that the shamans spoke to their spirits in a strange, squeaky voice. They also found among the tribes certain images of geese with extended wings, sometimes of brass. And here we are reminded that in Mal'ta, that paleolithic hunting station where no less than twenty female figurines have been discovered, a number of flying geese or ducks were also found, carved, like the figurines, in mammoth ivory."[8]

Brahma on a Cosmic Gander, painting from southern India

In India, Hindu master yogis "who in their trance states go beyond all the pales of thought, are known as *hamsas* and *paramahamsas:* 'wild ganders' and 'supreme wild ganders.' In the imagery of traditional Hinduism, the wild gander is symbolic of *brahman-atman,* the ultimate, transcendent yet immanent ground of all being, with which the yogi succeeds in identifying his consciousness, thus passing from the sphere of waking consciousness. . . to the nonconditioned, nondual state 'between two thoughts,' where the subject-object polarity is completely transcended and the distinction even between life and death is dissolved."[9]

Thus the gander serves as symbol for the supreme union of opposites, Brahman with Atman, the Infinite with the Finite, the individual soul with the Godhead. And it is in this connection that we see the Hindu God Brahma, the Creator, depicted riding on a Cosmic Gander (see illustration).

In early Egyptian mythology, the usual association of a male god with the sky and the female with the earth was curiously reversed. And so we find the sky personified as the Mother, Nut, who arches her body up and over the male earth god, Geb, who is both her brother and her husband. Geb was also represented as a gander (see illustration), and the couple was thought to unite in close embrace each night, as the darkness of the

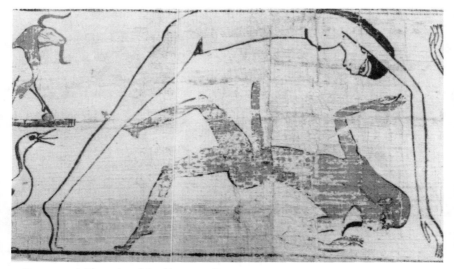

Papyrus of Tameniu, 21st Dynasty Egypt

night sky enveloped the earth. This reversal of sexual roles had some strange results: in his role as gander, Geb was called "The Great Cackler," and it was he who was thought to have laid the cosmic egg, from which the sun was born.

Many of these rituals and beliefs surrounding the goose have involved a similar association with the sun, and thus with fertility. In China a pair of geese was traditionally presented to the newly married couple. These associations may well have originated from the massive migrations of geese seen during the spring, which herald the "return of the sun," the lengthening days, and the beginning of the growing and mating seasons.

In Greece, of course, it was Aphrodite herself who rode on the goose (see cover and illustration on page 00). Aphrodite was goddess of love and beauty, among many other things, and filled the creative function of The Great Goddess, in that she symbolized the fertile and regenerative powers of nature, like the goose, in three realms: on land, in the sea, and in the air. She was a female ruling principle of Nature. And from the illustration we can imagine that she might almost be the one being described in the rhyme:

> Old Mother Goose, when
> She wanted to wander,
> Would ride through the air
> On a very fine Gander.[10]

51

Aphrodite riding on a goose, line drawing by the author, after Pistoxenus, painter, Attic cup, Greece, 500-475 B.C. (British Museum)

So here in several separate traditions we find the goose equated with transcendental flight, fertility, and the underground, and symbolizing a union of opposites. In three of the traditions—Indian, Egyptian, and Greek —we find the creative aspect of The Godhead represented as riding on or mating with a goose (or gander). Seen in this light, the humble and familiar figure of Mother Goose acquires unexpectedly divine company!

IV
Myth and Meaning

WHOEVER AND whatever else she may be, Mother Goose is the fictional caretaker and guide for a collection of literally hundreds of folk and fairy tales, riddles, and rhymes. Collectively they constitute an entire body of mythology for children.

Like the larger body of world myth, they serve to link the two worlds between which man lives, suspended. These are the Infinite and the finite realms of Heaven and earth, of spirit and flesh. If man lives between the two, the two worlds also live within him. Outwardly they are the heavenly and the earthly; inwardly, they are the unconscious and the conscious—the soul or psyche and the mind. Myth provides a pathway between the two levels of these inner and outer worlds.

"Myth" is a term too often used in a negative sense to refer to someone else's religion. But it may have two meanings: a fictitious story or a symbol for truth, in the Platonic sense of allegory. It is hard to imagine a more protean term. Yet fiction and truth are not exclusive. Any thoughtful reader knows that well-conceived fiction may reveal more of truth than waking reality may do. And most of us will admit that our waking "reality" often contains a good deal of fiction.

One of the best and simplest definitions of myth is Carl Jung's: "Myths are first and foremost psychic manifestations that represent the nature of the psyche.''[1] Joseph Campbell's is equally meaningful: ''Mythology is psychology, misread as cosmology, history and biography.''[2] In other words, the themes treated universally in myth do not describe external phenomena so much as they describe an internal state. The world of myth is a world of shadows, cast into consciousness by the forms that inhabit the unconscious. And the light which casts the shadows shines from deep within the soul. Here we are reminded of the teaching: Not Two and Not One—the world without and the world within, they are not separate, and not the same. As Campbell points out, ''even. . .the so called primitives, priests, wizards and visionaries interpret and re-interpret myth as symbolic of 'the Way': 'the Pollen Path of Beauty,' as it is called, for example, among the Navajo.''[3]

Another writer who has dealt extensively with myth is Mircea Eliade, who describes it both as ''an element of civilisation'' and ''an exemplary pattern of human behaviour.'' He further points out that ''at the level of *individual experience* it has never completely disappeared: it makes itself felt in the dreams, the fantasies, and the longings of the modern man; and an abundant psychological literature has now accustomed us to rediscoveries of both the big and the little mythologies in the unconscious and half-conscious activity of every individual.''[4] Eliade also makes a valuable distinction between what he calls the "Great Time," which is the sacred, holy, and "timeless" time referred to in myth and fable, and the more familiar "profane" and worldly or historical time of consciousness.

Again we face the duality: myth as the collective and outer correspondent to individual and inner dream; and myth and dream alike as expressive of the timeless and infinite, as opposed to the temporal and finite plane where we live out our waking and physical existence.

Aside from their outer and inner placement, how do myths and dreams differ? Jung explains that both contain similar themes or motifs—he calls them primordial images, or archetypes—but that in myth these themes appear in "an ordered and for the most part immediately understandable context,"[5] while dreams present "a generally unintelligible, irrational, not to say delirious sequence of images which nonetheless does not lack a certain hidden coherence."[6] Simply put, a myth is more readily understandable than a dream, though both deal with a similar set of archetypal images and themes. This is an important distinction, and one to which we will return.

The folk or fairy tale may be described as a lesser variant of myth, sharing similar concerns, but animated more by a desire to entertain than to provoke a state of religious awe. Campbell refers to the folk tale as "the primer of the picture-language of the soul,"[7] and Bruno Bettelheim describes fairy tales as works of art, "fully comprehensible to the child as no other form of art is."[8]

For a number of complex reasons, traditional myth has died for modern man and has become for him "only myth," that is, fiction. For Jung this death constitutes one of the greatest crises of modern existence. But if we can no longer give credence to Odin, to Zeus, and such figures, folk tales do survive and are augmented, modified, lost, reinvented, and passed on by each successive generation. In a sense the folk or fairy tale may be said to represent the dilution and democratization of myth. If the tales are less mighty, they are also more credible and more accessible to modern man.

The inner richness of the classic folk tale has been deeply appreciated by any number of writers and thinkers: the German poet Schiller wrote "deeper meaning resides in the fairy tales told to me in my childhood than in the truth that is taught by life."[9] It should be added that "literary critics such as G. K. Chesterton and C. S. Lewis felt that fairy tales are 'spiritual explorations' and hence 'the most life-like' since they reveal 'human life as seen, or felt, or divined from the inside.' "[10]

More recent authors—Jung, Campbell,

Eliade, and Bettelheim among them—have examined the psychological depths of symbolic meaning in fairy tales. Bettelheim has helped us to understand *The Uses of Enchantment.* in the psychological development of the child. But while the *tales* of Mother Goose have been so thoroughly probed, the nursery *rhymes* have not. Most of the scholarly interest in nursery rhyme (and there has been a great deal) occurred prior to the contributions and discoveries of modern depth psychology, and was restricted to the investigation of very limited and literal historical events, personalities, and precedents to which the rhymes might be traced. Very little has been done to examine the rhymes of Mother Goose in the same way that these authors and others have discussed the fairy tales.

Perhaps the simplest, most obvious, and most important distinction between the tales and the rhymes is that the tales are in prose form, meant to be told or to be read, while the rhymes are poetry, meant to be sung, or chanted. A second and less obvious difference is that fairy tales, like myths, are developed in a rather clear and serial narrative form, in an "ordered and for the most part immediately understandable context." They are intended for the adult and for the somewhat older child who has developed a large enough vocabulary and enough familiarity with the conscious world of time and causation to understand them. They are for the child who has a sufficiently lengthened attention span to follow the complexities of their relationships and development. Fairy tales are the mythology of middle childhood, and serve the psychic needs of that period, just as myth serves the psychic needs of the cultures in which it survives.

The nursery rhymes of Mother Goose, on the other hand, are the mythology of infancy and early childhood. Like dreams, they offer "a generally unintelligible, irrational, not to say delirious sequence of images which nonetheless does not lack a certain hidden coherence." Like aural lightning, they strike directly to their target in the unconscious of the young child, and operate outside the realm of orderly time and space, beyond causation. Their images and associations and the sequence of their events may be as nonsensical, irrational, and unlikely as those encountered in dreams. They depend only marginally on the concepts of an orderly and sensible world, and refer only superficially to the very simplest subjects and objects known to waking consciousness.

And quite properly so, since toddlers, who are their proper audience, are themselves only beginning to emerge into the world of consciousness. They are only barely and very imperfectly acquainted with its concepts of ordered time and space, its principle of causation, its notions of mortality and morality, and the subjects and the objects of its interest.

In brief, the difference between fairy tales and nursery rhymes is the difference between poetry and prose, with all that that implies. For this reason, we should consider something of the nature of rhyme in general before we begin to examine the particular and quite unique rhymes of Mother Goose.

Rhyme and Reason

A government publication regulating the manufacture of an automobile tire may require more than 100 pages to convey its message. The Golden Rule, on the other hand, is expressed in fewer than a dozen words, and Socrates' maxim, "Know Thyself," in only two.

Why is it that great wisdom and great simplicity so often seem to come hand in hand? Why are so many of the world's great religious scriptures poetic, while theology is prose? Why do the authors of the *Bhagavad Gita*, the *Tao Teh Ching*, and much of the Bible, like Shakespeare, choose to deliver their messages in a poetic fashion? Why must they sing, rather than simply say their words?

An obvious answer may be that of all the

forms of verbal expression poetry alone offers the greatest potential for economy of expression: it can transmit the maximum message with the most minimal means. Or, to put it another way, poetry can evoke the greatest inner richness through the greatest outer simplicity.*

Poetry clearly has a unique capacity for embodying the most profound, abstract, and ethereal ideas within the simplest, most intimate, and earthiest kinds of image and meter. Perhaps above all else it is the meter, the rhythm of the rhyme, that reverberates and echoes within us. For the rhythm of the rhyme repeats the rhythms of both our outer and our inner worlds: the very beat of our own hearts, the measured rate of our breathing, the pulse of the tides, the cycles of the days and seasons, the movements of the stars themselves—all of the internal and external rhythms of life—find a verbal counterpart in the rhythm of rhyme. In this sense, the highest forms of rhyme and of reason are not as unrelated as conventional wisdom would have it. It is no accident that some of our most inspired philosophers have expressed themselves like poets, and that our best poets are invariably philosophers as well.

---

*Of the visual forms of language—drawing, painting, and sculpture—drawing may most closely parallel this potential of poetry for ''saying most with least.''

If all of this seems a fanciful and highflown preface to the discussion of some simple and nonsensical nursery rhymes, it need not and should not. The very commonness and utter familiarity of these rhymes may have bred contempt in us. But the collection of rhymes which we attribute to Mother Goose may very well constitute one body of Western literature which has remained more intimately familiar to more people for a longer time than any other that we know.

Many of these rhymes actually bridge the gap between the oral and written traditions of our culture. Shakespeare certainly knew and recited some of them in his youth. If we are asked to recall and recite accurately from memory a single biblical proverb or nursery rhyme, what will spring most readily to mind for most of us? Through generation after generation, these rhymes have been recited, in virtually identical forms, by parents and children. Memorized complete in earliest childhood before we can read or even speak very well, they accompany us to our graves.

In a culture that discards best-selling novels and ''million-seller'' songs on a regular monthly basis, how may the incredible persistence and longevity of these nursery rhymes be satisfactorily explained? What is their function?

It has been pointed out that nursery rhymes constitute a mythology of infancy and early childhood; and that, like dreams, they offer an irrational sequence of images which have "a certain hidden coherence." It has been claimed that the rhymes may contain archetypal imagery drawn from the collective unconscious, and that they thereby serve the psychic needs of early childhood, just as *fairy tales* serve the needs of middle childhood, and myth serves in the cultures where it thrives. But this is a very broad definition of the functions of nursery rhyme. And of the 200 or so rhymes we associate with Mother Goose, certainly not all can be said to contain profound and hidden messages for the unconscious mind of the child. But we can accurately describe the rhymes as an initiatory body of literature for the very young.

In this capacity, the rhymes serve as an introduction to the concepts, values, and traditions—the very ways—of consciousness. Without attempting to construct a detailed catalog of all the lesser- and better-known rhymes, we may acknowledge that a great many of them accomplish this function within a clear and limited range.

Some of the rhymes simply introduce the child to the names of things, to numbers, letters, sounds, or colors—in short, to an orderly, and systematic way of perception and cognition. In this group, for example, would be rhymes such as "One, Two, Three," "The Alphabet," and "Five Toes." Other rhymes are tongue-twisters or riddles, based on obvious delight in playful sounds, rhythms, ideas, and associations. This group might include riddles such as "A Well," "The Mist," "Teeth and Gums." Some of these serve to help in the development of spoken language. Other rhymes are clearly meant as simple cautionary or moralistic lessons that introduce the child to an elementary system of values. Among these are "Tom, Tom, the Piper's Son," "For Want of a Nail," and "If Wishes Were Horses."

Some are counting-out rhymes that systematically serve, through their repetition, to introduce the child to a process of differentiation in which one thing or person is singled out from a group. Some are cumulative rhymes that build up a sequence of events, and thereby introduce the child to an orderly sense of time and space and to the principle of cause and effect—and even to the idea of mortality. There are still other rhymes that serve to acquaint the child with some of the common traditions, customs, manners, and mores of the culture.

In their separate ways, all of these various types of rhymes serve to initiate children into the ways of waking consciousness, and to escort them gently away from the undifferentiated perceptual flux, the random sense of space and time, the chaos of the unconscious state in which they live. Rhymes introduce children to the world of temporality, causation, differentiation, mortality, and morality, where they are destined to live.

Perhaps the most familiar example of the type of rhyme that traces a sequential and temporal relationship, the cumulative rhyme, is "The House That Jack Built," a lengthy story in which the rat eats the malt, the cat kills the rat, the dog worries the cat, and so on, until at last the forlorn maiden and the man "all tattered and torn" are married, by a priest who has been awakened by the crowing of a cock, which is owned by a farmer, etc. If there is a temporal relationship in all of this, however, it is a rather strange one that partakes as much of chance as of necessity. There is no clear causal relationship traced in the rhyme. Jack, who built the house, has absolutely nothing to do with any of it, except that his house serves as the starting point of the tale. One event does not clearly lead to the next in this long series of happenings. If there is any lesson in this, it is that we live in a world of randomness and chance, where things happen sequentially, to be sure, but without the kind of clear causality that is expressed in other rhymes of the same kind.

This type of cumulative rhyme is thought to have very ancient precedents that may be found in Hebrew chants of the sixteenth century and much earlier. There is a ritualistic quality about them, and a fatalism: one kind

of entity, force, or creature usually controls
the destiny of the next, and its fate is in turn
affected by another greater than itself, etc.
But it is not always an entirely rational world
that is reflected in such rhymes.

A far more orderly temporal sequence is
presented in other rhymes of this type, some
of which also deal with our own mortality, for
example:

I married a wife on Sunday,
She began to scold on Monday,
Bad she was on Tuesday,
Middling she was on Wednesday,
Worse she was on Thursday,
Dead was she on Friday;
Glad was I on Saturday night,
To bury my wife on Sunday.[12]

This ancient rhyme includes a hard-hearted
and pessimistic view of marriage, along with
its lesson on the days of the week. Charles
Lamb apparently enjoyed it so much that he
included copies of it, in Latin, in letters to
his friends.[13] Another orderly cumulative
rhyme is:

Solomon Grundy
Born on a Monday,
Christened on Tuesday,
Married on Wednesday,
Took ill on Thursday,
Worse on Friday,
Died on Saturday,

Buried on Sunday,
This is the end
of Solomon Grundy.[14]

This rhyme has a neat matter-of-factness, a complete lack of moralizing or piousness that children can understand, since they share its straightforward, blunt, and uncomplicated view of things. It is only adults who may be shocked easily. The rhyme presents the whole passage of life, from birth to death, in ten brief lines—what greater economy could we ask?

Some of the other rhymes of this type, which also deal with a sequence of events, include an element of ritual, so important to help children begin to arrange their own existence into the orderly patterns that are essential for participating in the world of consciousness. These patterns will soon be imposed upon children, whether or not they learn them by themselves. An example might be "One, Two, Buckle My Shoe." And loosely grouped within the same category we might place other well-known rhymes, such as "This Little Piggy Went to Market," "The Mulberry Bush," "The Mouse and the Clock."

However, it is not the purpose here to pursue any further classification of types and examples of rhymes and their uses. Any such attempt would clearly identify a great number of Mother Goose rhymes as filling some fairly clear and recognizable need in initiating the child into consciousness.

Any such attempt will also and inevitably turn up rhymes that are not so easily understood and not so easily classified according to their function. Among these must be placed some of the most ancient, most familiar and often repeated rhymes of all. By comparison to the ones just discussed, these favorite rhymes—"Hush a Bye, Baby," "Humpty Dumpty," "Mary Had A Little Lamb," "Little Bo-peep," and others—tend to be cryptic, irrational, nonsensical, and puzzling to the extreme. They are the subject of greatest interest, and the object of investigation in the following section.

V
The Rhymes

Hush a By Baby: The Tree of Life and Death

It is likely that the earliest form of nursery rhyme may have been the lullaby. For most children the first exposure to Mother Goose occurs in very early infancy, when the child is but a few days old, and first hears sung the best known lullaby in the English language:

> Hush a by Baby
>   On the Tree Top,
> When the Wind blows
>   The Cradle will rock;
> When the Bough breaks
>   The Cradle will fall,
> Down tumbles Baby,
>   Cradle and all.[1]

Like many of the rhymes, the exact origins of this lullaby are unclear. It is fair to say that it is at least several hundred years old. If we consider the words of the rhyme, it seems a curious and unpleasantly harsh thing to sing in order to comfort a tiny, defenseless, and restless infant. But of course when it is first used, the child is far too young to understand the words. It is rather the melody and the soothing rhythm of the rhyme that does its work.

75

Nonetheless, it is a curious story: a baby in a cradle on the top of a tree; the wind blows, and the cradle rocks to and fro; the limb breaks; the baby, the cradle "and all" tumble down.

The images used in the rhyme are quite simple and limited. Before they are toddlers, children will understand all of the principal words. At most, there are four images employed: the two primary ones of the baby and the tree (or more exactly, the tree *top*); and the secondary ones of the cradle and the wind. The action of the narrative, if we may call it that, is in three stages: the baby is first in the cradle on the tree top, then swinging or rocking as the wind blows, then falling and tumbling down when the bough breaks. It is a strange story. What meaning can it have?

Given the associations among nursery rhymes, fairy tales, myths, and dreams, and their connection with the archetypal images of the collective unconscious, the obvious place to begin any search for meaning is in the images and actions of the rhyme. If we begin with the image of the tree (or tree top) and its role in traditional myth, we will quickly discover an incredible wealth of symbolic association and usage, in the mythology of virtually any culture we may care to examine. An entire volume on the subject of the tree alone could easily result from such research.

In order to narrow our field of inquiry, we

76

The wak-wak tree with its human fruit, from A Turkish History of the West Indies, *Constantinople, 1730*

might restrict our search to mythical precedents for babies in tree tops, but even then we would be overwhelmed with the numbers and types of examples. In literally dozens of cultures, trees are represented in myth as birth-giving mothers. In Greek myth, ash trees are the mothers of the men of the Bronze Age. In Egyptian mythology, one version of the Great Mother is Hathor, who is represented as a sycamore tree which gives birth to Horus, the infant sun god.

In general, the tree in its mythical associations is most often equated with the Mother who nourishes, sustains, and transforms. "And the child bearing tree may be further differentiated into tree top and nest, crib and cradle. That is why the New Year's festival in Egypt is also called the 'day of the child in the nest,' while the birth of the day, as time of the sun's little birth, is essentially identical with the birth of the year as the sun's great birth."[2]

The archetypal tree is a Tree Of Life, and is thereby the central form of vegetation connected with The Great Goddess in her life-supporting and positive aspect: "the female nature of the tree is demonstrated in the fact that tree tops and trunk can give birth, as in the case of Adonis and many others."[3]

But if the tree is associated with the earth of Mother Nature and the physical fact of birth-giving, it is also a symbol of transcendence and psychic birth, or rebirth. In this connection, it is not only the Tree of Life or the Tree of the World, as it is known in primitive societies, but also the Tree of Heaven, the Cosmic Tree, rooted in the earth but reaching into the heavens and uniting the two. By linking the two realms, the tree serves in myth as a route of access into the Infinite, a ladder from earth to Heaven. In primitive cultures, "the celestial ascension of the shaman is contrived by means of a tree or post, which symbolizes the cosmic Tree or Pillar."[4] In this role, the tree is usually described as situated at the center of the world, a cosmic axis uniting the upper and lower worlds, and thus "in the mythic time of Paradise, a Mountain, a Tree or a Pillar or a liana connected Earth with Heaven, so that primordial man could easily go up into Heaven by climbing it."[5] Certainly there are many traditions in which the souls of the dead are described as climbing a mountain or a tree in their passage to the other world, as well.

In its function of providing a link between the two realms, the tree serves as a symbolic union of opposites. Thus it is to be expected that its association with the Great Mother is balanced in the myth of some cultures by a male and phallic connotation, as seen in the early Hindu sculptures of the Yakshi, an Indian version of the Mother, in which she is

Yakshi figure, from East gate, Great Stupa, Sanchi, India

depicted entwined intimately about the trunk of a fruit-bearing tree (see illustration).

The union of opposites embodied in the iconography of the tree has additional roots in the Christian use of the symbol, where the Tree of Life is also encountered as the Tree of Death, or the Cross on which Christ dies. In fact, both Christianity and Judaism employ the tree in these two contradictory and paradoxical forms. Christ hangs from the Tree of Death, but *is* the Tree of Life, and furthermore, "the tree of knowledge is identified with the tree of life and death that is the Cross."[6]

According to medieval Christian legend, Adam was buried on Golgotha, and "Seth planted on his grave a twig from the tree of Paradise, which grew into Christ's Cross, the Tree of Death."[7] This brings the biblical story full circle, from Genesis and the Creation to the Crucifixion: sin begins in the world with Adam's guilt when he eats from the Tree of Knowledge in the Garden, and Christ, through his death on the Tree, redeems us from this guilt. The Tree of Life begets the Tree of Death; Adam's sin begets Christ's expiation and crucifixion. There seems to be a terrible balance and inevitability at work here, a law of compensation, such as is described quite simply in the *Tao Teh Ching:*

Since the world points up beauty as such
There is ugliness too.
If goodness is taken as goodness,
Wickedness enters as well.
For is and is-not come together;
? — Hard and easy are complementary;
Long and short are relative;
High and low are comparative;
Pitch and sound make harmony;
Before and after are a sequence.[8]

The association in Christianity of the tree with both life and death is not unique, however. In Egyptian mythology, the tree is linked not only with Hathor, but with another model of the Great Mother, Nut, the coffin goddess.

If we jump quite suddenly now from the realm of the distant and mythical back into the realm of daily waking consciousness, which we all share, we will still find dim traces and echoes of some of the rich symbolism surrounding the tree. It is there in our traditions of May poles and Christmas trees, for example, and perhaps also in the fact that, at the beginning of each of our lives, we were most probably tucked into a cradle, traditionally hewn from a tree. At the end of our lives, we will most likely be tucked into a coffin, another version of the tree, before we are placed back into the earthen womb of the Mother.

Beginning with a simple if puzzling lullaby, we now find ourselves rather far afield. But that is most often the case with myth and dream, and nursery rhyme as well. An examination of any particular symbol may quickly widen, like the ripples from a stone dropped into a pond that soon cover the entire surface of the pond. The particular becomes the universal, the universal is rooted in the particular—they are Not Two and Not One, not separate and not the same. It is the lesson of the Tao.

What *possible* meaning can any of this have for a parent who sings the lullaby and for the infant who cannot yet even understand the words? Were the lullaby sung but once and forgotten, there would be no meaning at all. But it is not. It was sung to us by our mothers, and to them by theirs, and we sing it to our children, as they will to theirs. It is sung to each child not once, but over and over, until the child outgrows lullabies during the months when the infant becomes the toddler. In all of this repetition, perhaps a subtle subliminal message is relayed to the child— not a conscious one, certainly. Most parents could not explain the rhyme, and certainly no child could. But on the unconscious level, there is a message to be sure, and it is contained both in the imagery, with its great wealth of buried and traditional symbolic associations and meanings, and in the action of the rhyme.

The action describes three states. First, there is the security of the baby nestled in the cradle, in the "tree" of mother and family. Second, disturbance comes as the winds of change, growth, and desire stir, and the motions of consciousness begin to disturb this security. The child begins to establish a separate, conscious identity of its own. Third comes the Fall, the breaking away, the assertion of independence, which every child one day confronts. This means separation from the "tree" of family on one level, and from the Source on a greater level still. It is in this greater context that the child's fall may be seen as a fall from the sacred and heavenly into the worldly realm.

The rhyme may be understood on many levels, but even on a very literal one it may be taken as a parable describing three stages of early life. It encompasses infancy, middle childhood, and mature youth—roughly the ages from birth to twenty. Certainly for the child, the rhyme is a description of the present and a projection into the future; it is a tentative initiation into the world of consciousness, and a foreshadowing of every child's destiny.

rockabye meaning

84

Humpty Dumpty and the Cosmic Egg

Soon after leaving early infancy and out-growing lullabies, very young children are likely to hear and enjoy one of their first favorites among the nursery rhymes, "Humpty Dumpty." It is easily one of the most ancient that we know. While the earliest printed version of the rhyme did not appear until near the beginning of the nineteenth century, some scholars think its age should be measured in thousands of years. The rhyme is known in very much the same form in virtually every European and Scandinavian language.* It is explained routinely by nursery rhyme scholars as a simple riddle, referring to an egg.

But if the history of myth and the ideas of Jung, Frazer, Campbell, Eliade, and Bettelheim, among others, mean anything, "Humpty Dumpty" is a great deal more than a simple riddle. The central and archetypal image in the rhyme is of course the egg.

---

*For a thorough investigation of the rhyme's earliest and alternate versions, see *Comparative Studies in Nursery Rhymes* by Lina Eckenstein.

So we need to understand something of the traditional meaning of the egg to understand the message of the rhyme.

At the biological level, the egg is the very center and origin of individual human life. The basic form of the egg and its variations— the dome, the sphere, and their two-dimensional counterpart, the circle—all have a pleasingly smooth and self-contained completeness, which is readily sensed but which defies adequate verbal description. These forms have been used to symbolize wholeness in cosmogonies, religions, and philosophies, and as models in the arts, architecture, and sciences, from humanity's earliest beginnings.

To the unsophisticated and child-like eye, the sky itself is like the inside of a large blue bowl or the inside half of a giant egg. And so the house of man has a floor of earth, and for roof and walls, this great blue dome of the sky. As we have seen, this association was reflected in the Latin and Greek words for "house," which were synonymous with "dome." Similarly, "in ancient Italy, Syria, India and Islam the words for house, tent or primitive shelter...came to designate a dome or domical structure."[1]

Early domed structures in Egypt and Babylonia carried out the microcosmic association between the dome and the sky quite literally, with blue ceilings and painted or mosaic stars. The practice was preserved in countless early Christian tombs and churches. According to E. B. Smith, the words of a Syrian hymn "The Sougitha" present the domical structure of the *Hagia Sophia** both as "the image of God and as a replica for the Universe"; the hymn compares the structure's gold mosaics to "the firmament, with brilliant stars," and the four supporting arches to "the four sides of the world."[2]

Freud, in his analyses of dreams, was perhaps the first modern writer explicitly to present churches and chapels as symbols for the female vagina or womb, and he described the dream-act of entering such structures as symbolic of incest or of a return to the womb. He was perhaps not so far wrong if we read in his analyses a description of the human longing for the Oneness, the need to return to the Source or the Mother. Even the Catholic Church acknowledges and accepts the designation "Holy Mother Church."

The microcosmic adaptations of the domical or egg-like form in architecture are but reflections of a greater cosmic symbolism that has traditionally surrounded the egg. In early Vedic beliefs in India, the Rig-Veda names the unknown creator of all things *Pra-*

---

*The Church of the Holy Wisdom, or Santa Sophia, built for the emperor Justinian in Constantinople between 532 and 537 A.D.

japati, "Lord of Creation." He is described as the self-begotten egg, the cosmic egg, from which he hatches himself and all of the world of multiplicity. Thus the divine Oneness resides in a primordial egg, which splits into two parts—the lower silver half being the earth, the upper golden half the heavens.

In early Egyptian mythology, as noted earlier, the sun is described as being born from a cosmic egg, laid by the gander Geb. Tibetan Buddhism also employs the egg motif, and Plato used the egg as a symbol for cosmic birth-giver as well.

The Greeks and Romans also held a rich complex of ideas surrounding the classical *Omphalos,* a smoothly rounded and conically domed stone in the Temple of Apollo at Delphi. Among other things, the stone symbolized a collective and central point which united the earthly and the spiritual domains. A closely related notion was shared by the cult of the Dioskuri at the advent of Christianity. Their belief in a Celestial Helmet had its roots in an earlier Hittite culture. It envisioned a smoothly rounded whole with an upper, radiant half to which man aspires, and a lower half of darkness, which he inhabits, and from which he yearns to escape.

The great wealth of ritual beliefs and practices surrounding the same basic egg-like form is too extensive and diverse to cover further. But it should be noted that eggs (often

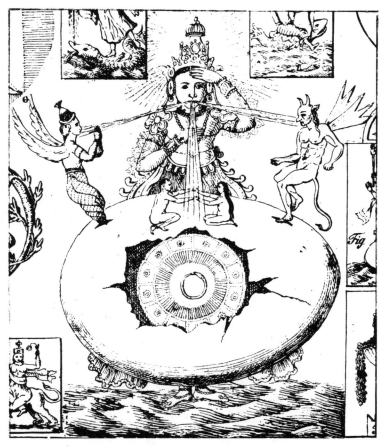

Prajapati with the world-egg, India, from Müller, Glauben, Wissen
und Kunst der alten Hindus, *Mainz, 1822*

brightly painted ones) were exchanged roughly at the time of the vernal equinox in Egypt, Persia, and China. Today the custom is preserved in European cultures as well as in America, where it has become curiously combined with the Easter bunny (significantly an underground creature), who brings the eggs. Each of these practices is bound up originally with the ideas of regeneration and renewal of the earth's fertility during the spring.

egg symbol today

Once again, this may seem a long way around to reach a simple nursery rhyme. But woven within the rich tapestry of these and related ideas may lie some tentative explanation for the long-lasting appeal and fascination of "Humpty Dumpty," the rhyme about the egg. In its most currently familiar form it goes:

> Humpty Dumpty sat on a wall.
> Humpty Dumpty had a great fall.
>   All the king's horses
>   And all the king's men
> Couldn't put Humpty together again.[3]

Examining the rhyme, a piece at a time, in the light of some of the egg symbolism that has been described, we first consider, "Humpty Dumpty sat on a wall." The egg, a symbol for wholeness and Oneness, sits atop a wall. Since any wall exists to separate two spaces, then from its vantage point on top of the wall, the egg obviously enjoys a command of both of these spaces. We may say that in the beginning there is a wholeness which governs two sides or two aspects—a Oneness, which oversees and unites the Two.

But then, "Humpty Dumpty had a great fall."

Like the baby's fall from the treetop, Humpty Dumpty's fall is from the holy and timeless into the historical and timely realm. Like the cosmic egg, Humpty Dumpty is fragmented: the wholeness is shattered, the One becomes the many, Unity becomes multiplicity. It is a "great fall" indeed, like the Fall of man from the grace of God, after which he finds himself outside the walled garden of Paradise. It is a disunion, a separation, a great loss.

The rhyme concludes;

All the king's horses
And all the king's men
Couldn't put Humpty together again.

"All the king's horses and all the king's men" may be interpreted in at least two ways. First and most obviously, they signify a total and collective effort by an organized force. In this sense the rhyme may be understood broadly as implying that all of humanity's collective and social efforts, the established institutions, the organized religions, will never be enough to restore us to our lost wholeness, our union with God. Such group efforts may allow the individual to overcome a sense of aloneness and separation, and may allow one to lose the individual self in the collective anonymity they provide.* But these afford only a superficial and symptomatic cure for estrangement from the greater wholeness which humanity seeks.

A second and similar sense in which the rhyme might be understood is that the horses and the men represent the two kinds of power of the king. Human personality is described similarly as having two kinds of power—the intuitive or emotive and the rational or intellectual. The horse has occasionally been used to symbolize each of these, but it is most commonly used in myth as an emblem for man's "bestial," lower, and darker powers, of the creative and intuitive unconscious. If that is the case here, then the men would have to represent the higher and more rational faculty. But neither of these forces can put Humpty together again. Even together they cannot effect a reintegration of the shattered whole.

---

*This may help to explain some of the great appeal and success of the various cults that insist on an absolute and uniform obedience in their followers.

92

In order to do that, one must transcend the duality of human personality, and achieve the integration of Kierkegaarde's "knight of faith"; one must become what the *Tao Teh Ching* calls "the Wise Man" or "the King."

If *all* of the horses and men cannot do it, then the reversed statement is also true: *none* (no-one) can do it. This may be understood in a positive sense, as described in the *Tao Teh Ching*. Speaking of the Wise Man, it says:

> His object is to restore everything to
> its natural course, but he dares take
> no steps to that end.
> Doing spoils it, grabbing misses it;
> so the Wise Man refrains from doing
> and doesn't spoil anything.[4]

> Indeed the Wise Man's office
> is to work by being still.[5]

> The Wise Man chooses to be last
> And so becomes the first of all;
> Denying self, he too is saved.[6]

This capacity of the Wise Man for "action-less action" results from self-denial, from the death of the personal ego, from becoming "no one." This psychological suicide, the death of the me, allows the Godhead, the Tao to work its wonders through me without my interference: None can do it. Still it can be done—when I become no one, the Wise Man, the knight of faith.

Here, expressed in capsule form for a child of two, is an introduction to the world of consciousness, of multiplicity and duality. Its fundamental lesson: "Child, your wholeness has been lost." And that is a lesson which the poet Wordsworth understood and taught to an older audience, in his "Ode: Intimations of Immortality":

Our birth is but a sleep and a forgetting:
The Soul that rises with us, our life's Star,
    Hath had elsewhere its setting,
        And cometh from afar:
    Not in entire forgetfulness,
    And not in utter nakedness,
But trailing clouds of glory do we come
    From God, who is our home:
Heaven lies about us in our infancy!
Shades of the prison-house begin to close
    Upon the growing Boy,
But He beholds the light, and whence it flows,
    He sees it in his joy;
The Youth, who daily farther from the east
    Must travel, still is Nature's Priest,
        And by the vision splendid
        Is on his way attended;
At length the Man perceives it die away,
And fade into the light of common day.[7]

Wordsworth envisions the infant as having just emerged from the Oneness ("From God, who is our home") and still living in its glow ("Heaven lies about us in our infancy!"). But he suggests that as the child grows older, he increasingly loses contact with the Source ("Shades of the prison-house begin to close..."), until finally "the Man perceives it die away,/And fade into the light of common day."

Perhaps, after all, the nursery rhyme scholars are right. "Humpty Dumpty" *is* a riddle—one that any child may profitably spend a lifetime solving. For many of us it will never be solved at all. It tells us first, "Your Oneness has been lost." This lesson alone may easily require half a lifetime in the learning, if it is ever learned at all. Second, it says, "All your gifts, your intellect, and your emotion—all your collective efforts—will not be enough to restore it. Put no faith in these."

This is the lesson learned by the knight of infinite resignation—that the Infinite and the finite are irreversibly and irreconcilably split apart. Yet there is still the exemplary knight of faith, the Wise Man, who somehow learns differently, and who is magically able to "put Humpty together again."

Mary Had a Little Lamb: A Song of Innocence

The rhyme "Mary had a little lamb" is a surprisingly modern one, and one of the few whose author is known; it was written in 1830 by Mrs. Sara Josepha Hale of Boston. Yet its symbolic associations and its message to the child are no less rich, well-founded, and meaningful than the more traditional rhymes.

> Mary had a little lamb,
> Its fleece was white as snow;
> And everywhere that Mary went
> The lamb was sure to go.
>
> It followed her to school one day,
> That was against the rule;
> It made the children laugh and play,
> To see a lamb in school.
>
> And so the teacher turned it out,
> But still it lingered near,
> And waited patiently about
> Till Mary did appear.
>
> Why does the lamb love Mary so?
> The eager children cry;
> Why, Mary loves the lamb, you know,
> The teacher did reply.[1]

This is a simple story, which a child of two can understand. The protagonists are Mary

96

and her lamb; the antagonists are the teacher and the school, and perhaps the other children as well. But the central image used in the rhyme is of course the lamb itself. This image is used in a number of Mother Goose rhymes which refer to lambs or sheep: "Little Boy Blue," "Little Bo-peep," "Bah, Bah a Black Sheep," and others.

Just as some of the traditional mythic and symbolic archetypes of the goose, the tree, and the egg have been traced, similarly some of the symbolic associations of the lamb or sheep must be known in order to understand these rhymes.

Like so many other animals, the lamb has been used allegorically in myth, folk tale, and religion, dating back into the blurred beginnings of civilization. Its symbolic usage is universally consistent with the actual character of the lamb itself, reflecting its gentle nature and its especially trusting character and habits.

Sculpted figures shown carrying a lamb or a calf were common in ancient Near Eastern civilizations, and in archaic and later periods of Greek culture. These were readily assimilated and adjusted to the needs of early Christian iconography, where we find the figure of Christ as the Good Shepherd, bearing a lamb on his shoulders. The image is clearly symbolic and lacks any historical associations, since Christ's father was a carpenter, not a herdsman, and there is no

Lamb of God, carved stone panel, chapel at Benoit-sur-Loire

biblical reference to the young Jesus serving as a shepherd-boy.

As seen earlier in the example of the Great Mother, the association of a god or a goddess with a particular animal, bird, or fish is quite common; the god or goddess may be presented either as accompanied by the creature or as embodied within the creature itself. Similarly, in Christian iconography we find Christ depicted not only as The Good Shepherd who bears the lamb, but as the very "lamb of God." He *is* the lamb, the holiness of God.

It is grimly ironic in this connection to note that the ritual sacrifice of lambs in pagan practice seems to have achieved its most awesome expression in the actual crucifixion of Christ, who by some accounts went gently, like a lamb, to his death.* That death was, for Christians, the expiation and abolishment of their sins, and so the Apocalypse shows the faithful washing their garments in the "blood of the Lamb."

This Christian use of the lamb symbol was later extended even further, so that the apostles also came to be depicted in early Christian art as lambs. The creature came to

*Not all accounts depict his death in this way. Consider the anguished cry, "My God, my God, why hast thou forsaken me?"

represent not only the unblemished purity of the essence of the Oneness, but the corresponding worldly and more limited human qualities and virtues of humility, holy simplicity, and patience.

All of these associations suggest that it is not entirely coincidence that the lamb in the rhyme should be associated with a female named Mary. But that may be a connection which is too tenuous to pursue further. We may accurately conclude, however, that the lamb was a well-established pre-Christian symbol; that it is a Christian symbol for Christ and represents the very essence of the holiness of God; and that similarly it may be taken as an emblem of the Oneness as it is manifest in each individual soul.

Aside from the more theological considerations, the nursery rhyme examined in its own light, tells us Mary has a lamb that accompanies her everywhere. When it goes to school with her, the other children are amazed, and the teacher turns it out. But the lamb waits for Mary until she emerges from school.

It is apparent that Mary has managed somehow to retain an original purity and innocence, ''as white as snow,'' something of the heaven which Wordsworth claims ''lies about us in our infancy,'' even up to the age of beginning school. Apparently most of the other children have lost this purity since, according to the rhyme, they are more or less astonished (but delighted!) to see such a thing in school.

The teacher and the school must represent the socializing influence of man's institutions, the world of waking consciousness, with its order, structure, causation, and dualities. Those of us who have passed through the school "system" know that it does not gladly countenance such things as lambs in school. It may serve to provide an environment for learning how to read and deal with numbers; it may socialize us and smooth out some of our more primitive tendencies. But it seldom nurtures our souls, or encourages the kind of creative quietude found in daydreaming, which may very well be the child's equivalent of adult meditation practices. Nor does the school look with favor on the nonpurposeful and unstructured sense of time and space that children bring to their first classrooms.

Indeed those "shades of the prison-house" that begin to close upon the growing child in Wordsworth's poem are all too frequently synonymous with the shades of the classroom (though in fairness to teachers, it should be noted that in the last stanza of the rhyme Mary's teacher does exhibit a degree of sympathy and understanding). If school is something of a prison, then the rhyme may contain a lesson for educators as well as for children.

Mary is a singularly gifted child whose "lamb" has not yet fled into the dark recesses of her unconscious, to become a shadowy animus encountered only in her dreams. We are assured by the rhyme that the lamb "waited patiently till Mary did appear." This may be rare, but it is not unheard of. Certainly we have all, at times, encountered in some rare individual—or in the work of an inspired artist, poet, philosopher, or scientist—the freshness, creativity, and purity of vision of childhood. The *Tao Teh Ching* refers to this simplicity, wonder, and spirit of awe: "Wise men hear and see as little children do."[2] It is unfortunate that our educations should so often serve to frustrate rather than to develop such unique vision and creativity.

Like "Hush a bye, Baby" and "Humpty Dumpty," Mary and her lamb may be teaching the child, in a completely disguised and subliminal way, that the loss of wholeness is at hand. If anything, Mary and her lamb offer the more positive version of the lesson, in that they suggest to the child that this impending initiation into the exclusive world of waking consciousness will not necessarily prohibit or deny the possibility of an eventual return to the Source. If we are as fortunate (or perhaps as determined) as Mary, we too may yet find our lambs waiting when we finish with school.

102

Little Bo-peep and Wu Wei

Little Bo-peep has lost her sheep,
  And can't tell where to find them:
Let them alone, and they'll come home,
  And bring their tails behind them.

Little Bo-peep fell fast asleep,
  And dreamt she heard them bleating:
But when she awoke, she found it a joke,
  For they were still all fleeting.

Then up she took her little crook,
  Determin'd for to find them;
She found them indeed, but it made her heart
    bleed,
  For they'd left all their tails behind 'em.

It happen'd one day, as Bo-peep did stray,
  Into a meadow hard by;
That she espy'd their tails side by side,
  All hung on a tree to dry.

She heav'd a sigh, and wip'd her eye,
  And over the hills went stump-o,
And tried what she cou'd, as a shepherdess
    shou'd,
  To tack each again to its rump-o.[1]

Carl Jung used the archetypal images contained in world myth to help elucidate and verify the significance and importance of dreams, as expressions of the collective unconscious. But his path is one that can be traveled equally well in either direction, now that it has been so well established. If these nursery rhymes are, as claimed, another and different form of myth, somewhat similar to dreams, their validity can be established by referring them to an established body of myth and archetypal images—as we have done in considering the previous rhymes. But their roots in the unconscious can also be shown by translating them into the language of dreams as related by a hypothetical dreamer, who in this example takes the place of Little Bo-peep:

I dreamed that I was in charge of taking care of a flock of sheep, but somehow I had lost them, and I had no idea what to do about it. I fell asleep and dreamed I could hear them, but when I woke up (in the dream) they were still missing.

Finally I just got desperately determined to find the sheep, and I set out to look for them. And I did find them, but all of their tails were gone. I was very sad, heartbroken about it.

Then I was wandering around, and I went into this meadow, and there was a tree there, and I saw all of the sheep's tails, hanging on this tree.

It made me kind of sad or resigned some-how, but I took all of the tails down, and went back to the sheep, to see what I could do about fastening them back on, and fixing the sheep up like they were supposed to be.

The rhyme very convincingly translates into the language of dream. The imagery and the sequence of events have about them something of the curious simplicity and irrationality of a dream. And we are left in a strangely suspended state by the tale told in this way; it has the tantalizing unclearness and inconclusiveness, the pungent scent of buried meaning, that we experience on waking after such a dream.

Surprisingly, the rhyme "Little Bo-peep" does not seem to have appeared in print prior to 1810. There is, however, a game "bo-peep" mentioned as early as 1364. We have all played it as infants and perhaps as parents or grandparents as well. Adults hide their faces (or the child's) then quickly reappear, saying "bo-peep!" (in the earlier version) or, as we are now more likely to say, "peek-a-boo!" This almost never fails to elicit startled and laughing delight in the very young child; and at a later age, the child will play "hide-and-go-seek," a slightly more sophisticated variation on the theme of loss and rediscovery. This theme is common to both games, and to the rhyme as well, and we will return to it.

First though, consider the images and the action of the story told in "Little Bo-peep." If the central image in "Mary Had a Little Lamb" was the lamb, certainly the central image in this rhyme is the sheep. All that has been said about the symbolism of the lamb applies equally well to the sheep here. They represent the instinctive forces within the unconscious, the holy aspect within the soul.

A difference between the two rhymes, however, is that Mary has one lamb, or baby sheep, with which she is virtually inseparable, while Bo-peep has a flock of sheep, and is a shepherdess responsible for their care. Mary loses her lamb through no fault of her own, but Bo-peep apparently loses hers through her own inattentiveness or carelessness. The differences between the two figures are clear: Mary is somehow the more infantile of the two, and indeed that rhyme, in its comparative simplicity, seems more suited to the younger child. Mary and her ''lamb''—her soul or psyche—are one. She has not yet fully emerged into the world of waking consciousness.

Bo-peep, on the other hand, is more grown up, more responsible, more clearly *separate* from her sheep. She is the shepherdess, with the responsibility for nurturing the instinctive and buried forces within the unconscious, just as Christ is the shepherd of our souls. She has lost them, and is upset by the loss.

Perhaps the most curious thing about the rhyme is the second half of the first stanza:

> Let them alone, and they'll come home,
> And bring their tails behind them.

These two lines are not a part of the narrative, as are all of the other lines of the rhyme. They are an interposition, more like a word of advice to Bo-peep inserted parenthetically into the story by the teller of the tale, perhaps by "Mother Goose" herself. And the advice they contain is paralleled precisely in the *Tao Teh Ching* in the concept of *wu wei,* actionless activity, creative quietude, or noninterference with the workings of the Tao. It means to do without doing, to be quiet and still so that the motion of the Tao may flow through you. In Christian terms, this is expressed as being at one with the will of God. The lesson is repeated in many of the verses of the *Tao Teh Ching:*

> The Way is always still, at rest
> And yet does everything that's done.
> (verse 37)
>
> Act in repose.
>   (verse 63)
>
> The world is won by refraining.
> (verse 57)
>
> By letting go, it all gets done;
> The world is won by those who let it go!
> But when you try and try,
> The world is then beyond the winning.
> (verse 48)

leave them alone + they will come home

The clue to the sheep's location nearby is revealed to Bo-peep in her dream—they are literally hidden in her own unconscious. But being somewhat grown up, she now lives predominantly in the world of waking consciousness; she ignores the dream, as she ignores the advice in the first stanza. She sets out "Determin'd for to find them," and so she does. But they are incomplete, mutilated through her own willfulness. This is a common and familiar theme in Greek tragedy, and one described quite simply by the *Tao Teh Ching*.

> People are constantly spoiling a project when it lacks only a step to completion.
>
> (verse 64)

Who among us has not experienced the truth of this firsthand, when we have prematurely forced a project or a situation to its conclusion, and then been dismayed, like Bo-peep, at the results?

Bo-peep was not able to find the missing parts of the sheep until "It happen'd one day, as Bo-peep did stray"—that is, when she allowed things to develop in their own way. She wandered, purposelessly, into a meadow, and there on the tree (the Tree of Life?) she found the missing elements. Saddened—perhaps by a mature understanding that her charges had been lost and mutilated through her own doing—but wiser now, she returns to her sheep, and tries to restore them to their proper state, that is, tries to repair her neglected and abused soul.

The central theme of the rhyme, and the message it brings to the unconscious mind of the child, is one of loss and rediscovery. Growing up and entering the world of waking consciousness necessitates a breaking away, a disunion, a loss of the Source, the One. But the instinctive forces of the unconscious, the soul, still live within us. And if we learn the lesson of Bo-peep, the lesson of *wu wei*, we may still find our "lost sheep," whole and complete, hidden where they have been all along—within ourselves.

Little Boy Blue:
The Divine Child

Apparently the archetypal figures of sheep and shepherds or shepherdesses are as popular and prevalent in nursery rhyme as in traditional myth and religion. Another example, this time a boy, is described in the rhyme "Little Boy Blue." As is common with many of the more familiar Mother Goose Rhymes, its origins are obscure. One nursery rhyme historian describes it as referring to Thomas, Cardinal Wolsey (1475?-1530), and *The Oxford Dictionary of Nursery Rhymes* suggests that it may derive from a passage in *King Lear* (Act III, Scene 6, lines 41-44).

Whatever its literal and historical associations may have been, the rhyme is contained in the earliest extant book of nursery rhymes, *Tommy Thumb's Pretty Song Book, Vol. II,* a single surviving copy of which now resides in the British Museum. The traditional version of the rhyme runs as follows:

Little Boy Blue, come blow your horn,
The cow's in the meadow, the sheep in the
    corn:
But where is the little boy tending the sheep?
He's under the hay-cock fast asleep.

110

Will you wake him? No, not I,
For if I do, he's sure to cry.[1]

It may be useful to follow the same scheme with this rhyme that was used with Little Bo-peep, that is, to translate and retell the story, in the format and language of a dream:

> I was on a farm in the country and we (I'm not sure who the others were) were all looking for a little shepherd boy. There were cows, which had gotten into a meadow, and some sheep had strayed into a cornfield where they weren't supposed to be, and we needed the little boy to control them. He was dressed all in blue, and had a special sort of horn—maybe a trumpet or a bugle, something like that, which he could use to summon the animals. But we couldn't find him. At last someone said that he was asleep under a big haystack there, and asked me to wake him up. But I didn't—I was afraid to, because I knew he would cry.

Once again, we may be struck by the ease with which the rhyme can be translated convincingly into a series of curiously dream-like images and events. But before we attempt to interpret the "dream," it is important to trace some of the archetypal images employed and their mythical precedents.

In addition to the basic symbolism of the sheep and shepherd, elements added in this

111

rhyme include the fact that the shepherd-child is male, is associated with the color blue, carries a horn of some kind, and lies sleeping beneath a haystack. Consider these elements singly, beginning with the color blue.

The symbolic use of particular colors in different cultures is a fascinating and a confusing study. Plato, St. Augustine, and Pliny each had theories regarding color, as have a great number of more modern writers, aestheticians, and color psychologists. Complex systems of conventional and symbolic color usage have been established in the traditional art forms of a great many widely separated cultures. But the same color does not always carry an identical or even equivalent meaning in these systems.

Within the Christian tradition alone there is confusion and contradiction. Yellow, for example, might signify glory when worn by St. Peter or Joseph in Medieval Christian art, but could mean cowardice when worn by Judas. Red could mean divine love when worn by St. John the Evangelist, and sin when associated with Satan.

Fortunately, in the Christian tradition at least, there is no such confusion about the color blue. Being the color of the sky, and therefore the color of the heavenly as opposed to earthly plane, it is used in Christian art as the color of heaven, spiritual love, truth, the divine. In Medieval art it was used exclusive-

ly for the robe of Mary, and thus clearly differentiated her from other more earthly
female mortals. The horn that Little Boy Blue
carries is clearly a mark of his authority as a
shepherd over the animals. And the animals
themselves are traditionally symbolic of the
creative, instinctive, and divine forces within
the soul.

While haystacks are not often mentioned in
myth, the related idea of the mound or hill is
quite common. In this connection the haystack (which, significantly, is a source of
nourishment for the animals) may serve as a
lesser version of the cosmic mountain which,
like the cosmic tree, serves to unite the
heavenly and earthly two. It is important to
note that in the rhyme Little Boy Blue lies
sleeping not beside or upon, but *under* the
haystack, and is thus presumably buried,
completely hidden from view.

Each of these elements and ideas is completely consistent with the archetype of the
divine child, who sleeps, buried within the
unconscious. This child-god archetype
expresses, according to Jung, "the all-
embracing nature of psychic wholeness," and
"symbolizes the pre-conscious and the post-
conscious essence of man."[2] In his extensive
investigation of this primordial figure, Jung
further notes that "the child is all that is
abandoned and exposed and at the same time
divinely powerful; the insignificant, dubious

113

beginning, and the triumphal end. The 'eternal child' in man is an indescribable experience, an incongruity, a handicap, and a divine prerogative; an imponderable that determines the ultimate worth or worthlessness of a personality.''[3]

It is significant that in the rhyme the location of this "sleeping savior" is clearly known. But when asked to awaken him, our hypothetical dreamer refuses, fearing the result. This reluctance is understandable. The difficulties, even the psychic dangers, involved in awakening the divine child within are described symbolically in world myth, and quite literally in the literature of mysticism, which warns in some detail of the kind of risks and dangers that may be encountered on the path into the unknown.

If there is some validity in any of these mythical associations, if in fact Little Boy Blue is unconsciously rooted in the primordial image of the divine child, then what is the meaning of the rhyme? It is a description of the sleeping savior and his function as shepherd of the instinctive forces within the soul; an identification of his location, buried within the unconscious; and a gentle warning of the difficulties that may be encountered in awakening him.

Quite obviously, children of three will not consciously grasp any of this. Nor would they understand if it could be explained. But they will absorb the central message of the rhyme: that everyone is looking for a very special child who is the only one capable of controlling the animals. They will sense that this child (and by extension, any child—even themselves) has extraordinary powers that even adults may lack. Further, they will be instructed that this special child is not inaccessible—his whereabouts is known. He is "sleeping under the haystack."

All of this taken together may provide a comforting assurance of the child's specialness, however buried and unawakened. The divine child and the forces he controls—the creative and divine elements within the soul—reside in each of us. They are there for anyone who may care enough, or dare enough, to awaken them.

Peter, his Pumpkin, and his Wives

The common theme central to all of the rhymes discussed is that of loss; a fall, fragmentation, or a separation from a divine wholeness is described in each. The baby falls from the tree of life, the cosmic egg is shattered, Mary and Bo-peep lose their lambs, the divine child is missing when most needed. The first two rhymes—"Hush a bye, Baby" and "Humpty Dumpty"—also describe the loss, but present the possibility of rediscovery as well: Mary's lamb waits patiently, Bo-peep finds her missing sheep and even their missing tails; and the whereabouts of Little Boy Blue is discovered, though there is some hesitation about waking him.

The importance of this kind of repetition for learning in early childhood should be apparent. Not only is each of these familiar rhymes recited repeatedly, both for and by the child, but the central themes are duplicated and re-encountered, in slightly altered forms, in the different rhymes. In each of the five rhymes, the action has evolved around a single central figure, a hero or heroine: the baby, the egg, the three shepherd figures.

In the next two rhymes, both well-known favorites as well, this basic format is changed.

Peter, Pumpkin Eater, from The Real Mother Goose, *by Blanche Fisher Wright*

We are presented not with one central figure, but with two—a male and female pair who share more or less equally in the action of the stories.

The first describes Peter, the pumpkin eater, and his two wives:

Peter, Peter, pumpkin eater,
Had a wife and couldn't keep her;
He put her in a pumpkin shell
And there he kept her very well.

Peter, Peter, pumpkin eater,
Had another, and didn't love her;
Peter learned to read and spell,
And then he loved her very well.[1]

The second stanza of the rhyme is not well known, but is a part of the traditional rhyme, and is completely essential to its full meaning, as will be seen.

This rhyme, like others earlier, may be translated easily and convincingly into a first-person narrative, and thereby achieves a truly dream-like quality:

I dreamed that I was married, but it grew increasingly difficult to keep track of my wife, to keep her with me. Finally I put her inside the hollow shell of a pumpkin I had been eating, and then it was all right.

I had another wife in my dream as well, and I didn't love her at all. But then I began learning how to read and to spell and I found that I began to love her after all.

118

This is a curious and seemingly nonsensical story, on the face of it. But we must remember our discussion of the anima, the animus, the complementary opposites of the male-female duality, and the symbolic significance of marriage. Each of Peter's wives is but a different aspect of himself. The first one is elusive, until she is confined. The second is not very lovable, at least until Peter begins learning to read and spell.

The central symbolic key to understanding the rhyme lies in the image of the pumpkin, which not only forms the basis of Peter's diet, but which serves to confine his elusive wife. Precedents for pumpkins in traditional myth are somewhat hard to come by, but there are popular customs, fairy tales, and fables that involve pumpkins, and in all of these the pumpkin has a basically similar meaning.

The traditional jack-o'-lantern, carved from a pumpkin for Hallowe'en at the end of the fall harvest, represents a friendly and beneficent spirit who will frighten away the evil and demonic forces who might be stalking the night.

Cinderella, which is probably the best known and best loved fairy tale of all, also deals with the image of the pumpkin. The story is very old, first written down in China in the ninth century. Its Oriental origin is still evident in the tale's concern with a tiny foot-size as indicative of special virtue and beauty. That association has never been a Western one, but was traditional in parts of the Orient, where mothers once even went so far as to bind the feet of girl babies, so as to insure a properly diminutive and beautiful foot.

The basic story of Cinderella has been told in a great number of forms throughout all of Europe and Scandinavia, in Africa, and in Asia. Bruno Bettelheim discusses and interprets the tale thoroughly in his book *The Uses of Enchantment.* [2] In the earlier versions of the tale, Cinderella's ultimate transformation is accomplished through the intervention of a Great Mother figure in the form of her own dead mother, who is manifest in an animal or vegetal form as a cow or a tree. This equation of animal and vegetal forms with the Great Mother is familiar, as discussed regarding the Great Goddess.

A somewhat more modern version of the tale, as told by Charles Perrault, a seventeenth-century fairy tale writer, was used as the basis for the Disney film of Cinderella. In this version the Great Mother appears out of nowhere as a fairy godmother, requests a pumpkin from the garden, scoops it out herself, and transforms it into a coach to transport Cinderella to the ball. It is there of course that Cinderella finds her own completion and wholeness in the figure of the handsome prince, who is the first mortal to recognize her inherent virtue and beauty.

Though not quite a tree, in this version of the tale the pumpkin also represents a vegetal extension of the Great Mother. It is used symbolically as the vehicle of transport that carries Cinderella into the realm of the other world, away from her drab waking reality and into her own unconscious, where she discovers her own integration and wholeness waiting.

Thus the pumpkin appears in the story of Cinderella as representative of both the beneficent aspect of the Great Mother and the forces of the unconscious. In more contemporary "myth," the pumpkin also appears in a form consistent with this traditional usage. The well-known cartoonist Charles Schulz created the idea of the Great Pumpkin, which in recent years has been enjoyed and accepted widely. Like Santa Claus, Schulz's Great Pumpkin is a purely beneficent representative from the realm of fantasy and the unknown.

In our rhyme, Peter *eats* pumpkins. Like the lotus for the lotus-eaters, the pumpkin provides his nourishment in both a real and a symbolic fashion. He is thus linked intimately with his own unconscious. But his wife, who also represents the instinctive and creative forces of his own unconscious, becomes increasingly elusive and difficult to keep track of, until he at last solves the problem by enclosing her within the shell or outward container of the pumpkin. She is thus in her rightful place in the unconscious.

His second wife, whom he does not love, represents another aspect of Peter, his budding but undeveloped consciousness. It is only after he begins his initiation into the orderly world of rationality by learning to read and to spell that he begins to accept and to value this aspect of himself.

In summary, then, Peter is like a child in a partially unconscious and preconscious state. But as he develops, the slippery, ungraspable, and unfixed qualities of the unconscious become increasingly elusive, until he chooses to confine this aspect of himself to a separate area within himself, the unconscious, and to begin his initiation into consciousness by exercising his rational and intellectual faculties. Then he finds that consciousness has its allures, as does the unconscious.

The meaning for the child in all of this is much the same as in the previous rhymes. A loss is described, but here it is because Peter chooses (as the child must eventually choose) to contain this element of himself within the unconscious, to enclose it or repress it. Peter, like the child, must begin his initiation into the ways of consciousness.

Jack and Jill and Yin and Yang

The last of the rhymes to be examined singly and in any depth is the one about Jack and Jill. Taken literally, it is a story of the boy and girl who go to get some water, and the literal bases of these rhymes may deserve more attention than we have thus far given them. We must remember that, for the most part, these rhymes are very, very old, and that many of the actual customs and practices they reflect are no longer our own.

For example, the lullaby, "Hush a bye, Baby," which was discussed on a purely symbolic level, describes a baby in a tree. Without denying the rhyme's symbolic associations or its connection with other mythical precedents, we should acknowledge that it was at one time a fairly common (and sensible) practice for a farm mother to sling her baby's cradle from the lower branches of a tree—in the shade, and away from insects on the ground—while she worked nearby. Early settlers in America saw Indian women do so, hanging their babies in birch-bark cradles, so that the wind might rock them while the mother worked. The *Book of Days* describes how female workers in the hop fields once slung their babies' cradles from the "hop-bines."[1]

Similarly, regarding other rhymes, it was quite common in an earlier period of our history for boys and girls to be pressed into service at quite an early age as shepherds for the family's flock. Finally, in the case of Jack and Jill, we should recall that the daily tasks of bringing in wood and water from the well once fell regularly to the younger children in a family, who were spared the heavier chores. This practice may have contributed to the literal basis of the rhyme.

The rhymes being grounded in actual custom was most important, in that it allowed the young child of an earlier era to recognize and identify more readily with the action of the rhymes. Naturally, none of this is directly applicable to the modern child. The fact that we continue to find something appropriate and relevant in these rhymes is due more to the accuracy of their symbolic content than to their reflection of any current custom.

Nonetheless, the symbolic values and the factual practices embodied in myth, tales, and nursery rhyme alike are not unrelated, but are bound as intimately together as, for instance, the actual character and the symbolic applications of the lamb.

The concrete and the abstract aspects of the rhymes confirm and strengthen rather than contradict one another. When any analysis of myths and rhymes grows too extreme and theoretical, it is important to be reminded of this fact.

"Jack and Jill" is one of the oldest rhymes of all. Some authorities trace it to an ancient Scandinavian saga about Hjuki and Bil, two children who are carried away from the earth by Mani, a "man in the moon," as they return from a spring carrying a bucket of water. As to the meaning of the rhyme, one scholar claims quite confidently that "the rhyme of Jack and Jill is a myth of the tides. And it happens that in this case we can trace the literary descent of the myth, so that it is not a matter of conjecture at all."* He points out that "Hjuki is derived from a root meaning *to increase,* Bil from one meaning *to dissolve,* and they represent the waxing and waning phases of the moon. The water they bear marks the relation of the tides to the moon—a relation that must have been noticed from very early times."[2]

This is all very well, but perhaps we will

---

*Other scholars, obviously less familiar with Scandinavian legend, have suggested alternate explanations; among them, one identifies Jack and Jill with the figures of two priests, Cardinal Wolsey and Bishop Tarbes, and relates the rhyme to their efforts to arrange a marriage for Mary Tudor.

be excused if we ask what exactly a "myth of the tides" refers to in human terms, in consciousness or unconsciousness. Maybe it is best to leave the interpretation aside while consulting the earliest known printed version of the rhyme, published about 1760 in *Mother Goose's Melody* by John Newberry and Oliver Goldsmith:

Jack and Gill
Went up the Hill,
  To fetch a Pail of Water;
Jack fell down
And broke his Crown,
  And Gill came tumbling after.

Up Jack got, and home did trot,
  As fast as he could caper,
To old Dame Dob, who patched his nob,
  With vinegar and brown paper.

When Gill came in, how she did grin,
  To see Jack's paper plaster;
Dame Dob, vexed, did whip her next
  For causing Jack's disaster.[3]

As in the rhyme about Peter the pumpkin-eater and his wives, this rhyme centers not on a single hero or heroine, but on a male and female pair. It may be helpful to translate this rhyme, as has been done with others, into the first-person prose narration of a dream. In this instance a male dreamer is arbitrarily assigned to recount the tale, as follows:

126

I dreamed that I was with a girl and we were climbing up a hill, to get some water from the top. On the way up, I fell and hurt my head, and when I fell, the girl did too. I got up and ran away to an old lady. She was bandaging my head and taking care of me, when the girl showed up and began laughing at me. But the old woman spanked her, and said it was all her fault that I had fallen.

It is very characteristic of a dream, and just as difficult to unravel. Several rather simple and matter-of-fact images are combined in a cryptic series of unexplained relationships and actions, to produce a puzzling story. Who are these two and what is their relationship? Why do they go for water? What is water doing at the top of a hill? Who is the old woman, and why does she punish Jill in this seemingly undeserved way?

The pair is involved in a joint task, obviously. A hill is a most unusual location for a water source, and as Lewis Spence points out, "no one in the folk-lore sense climbs to the top of a hill for water unless that water has special significance."[4]

It must be very special water and a very special hill. Symbolically in myth and in religion, water conventionally refers to the divine forces within the Tao, the Godhead, the soul, or the unconscious. The verses of the *Tao Teh Ching* repeatedly use water as a central symbol for the Tao itself:

A deep pool it is,
Never to run dry.
      (verse 4)

The reason for the analogy is explained:

Nothing is weaker than water,
But when it attacks something hard
Or resistant, then nothing withstands it,
And nothing will alter its way.
      (verse 78)

In Christian symbolism, water is used in a similar sense. The most obvious and familiar evidence of this is found in the baptismal practices common to both the Catholic and Protestant faiths, which use real or symbolic immersion to symbolize spiritual rebirth.

In myth, as Erich Neumann points out, water is "the primordial womb of life, from which in innumerable myths life is born."[5] He adds that "it is no accident that in fairy tales a well is often the gate to the under-world and specifically to the domain of the earth mother. . ."[6] This connection between water and the intuitive, feminine aspect of the creative unconscious is similarly common in dreams, where themes involving wading, swimming, drowning, in a sea, a lake, river, or pond abound.

In myth, religion, and fairy tales, a hill or mountain (and the idea of ascent) also involves a spiritual connotation, as it affords a connecting link, an upward path, between the earthly and heavenly realms.

In the light of these associations, it is likely that Jack and Jill, the male and female pair, may symbolize fundamental male and female principles, mutually necessary but opposite forces, which must come together, like Yin and Yang, to form and complete the Oneness. If their names derive from root words meaning "to increase" and "to dissolve," that merely strengthens the possibility that these two represent opposite and complementary forces, a fundamental dualism. If that supposition is accurate, then the rhyme may be read as a symbolic expression of the Two yearning for the One, the duality of the male and female principles striving upward toward integration and divine union. This interpretation need not conflict in any fundamental way with the scholar's insistence that the rhyme is a "myth of the tides." It merely enlarges and enriches the idea of the waxing and waning processes, explains them in a larger context as opposing and complementary movements within the one great "sea of the unconscious."

However, the two fail in their ascent: Jack falls and breaks his "crown"* and (in-

---

*It should be noted that the *crown* of the head has a special religious and secular significance, attested to by the shaven tonsures of medieval monks, the wearing of the *yarmulke* by males, in Judaism, and the crowns worn by rulers in traditional kingships. In yogic practice the crown of the head is identified with the highest center of consciousness.

evitably) Jill comes "tumbling after." Then Jack leaves Jill and flees to the old woman, who displays all of the benevolent and protective solicitude of a mother toward Jack. But when Jill shows up and begins to tease, the old woman whips her "for causing Jack's disaster." On the literal, surface level, Jack sounds suspiciously like a "mama's boy," and the antipathy between the old woman and Jill, though unexplained, sounds uncomfortably like that between an overzealous mother and her new daughter-in-law. Could Jill and Dame Dob represent two opposing and conflicting aspects of the same feminine principle, each competing for control of Jack's affections and his destiny? It is an obscure and difficult rhyme, and perhaps it is just as well to attempt no further interpretation. Things of real importance may suffer from too much explanation and be lost or ruined in the process.

Still, one wonders about the significance of the rhyme for a child. On either a literal or a symbolic level, the rhyme describes an ascent, a mission or a search, a failure, and a return. It presents the goal of the pair and describes allegorically a great ascent and adventure which lies ahead for the child. Yet simultaneously, the rhyme contains an assurance for the child that, should he fail in his first awkward steps on this journey, there will always be the solace and security of his mother's care, awaiting his return. It is not simple, nor is it an inappropriate message for the beginning of life. It is a profound teaching about the nature of duality and the search for wholeness, both reminiscent and worthy of the *Tao Teh Ching*.

"Peter, the Pumpkin Eater" and "Jack and Jill" are probably the best examples of nursery rhymes that deal with complementary male and female characters. But they are not the only ones; other examples include the rhyme about Jack Sprat (who could eat no fat) and his wife (who could eat no lean), and how "betwixt them both, they lick'd the platter clean."[7] A similar theme is expressed in the very ancient and popular rhyme titled "Cock a Doodle Doo," which tells of the incomplete Dame (who's lost her shoe, like Cinderella) and the incomplete Master (who's lost his fiddle stick). This rhyme concludes with each of them finding what they have lost, so that the pair is complete, the Dame dancing while the Master fiddles.

Without discussing the particular symbolism involved in these rhymes (eating, dancing, and making music, the plate, the shoe, the fiddle stick), it should nevertheless be readily apparent that each is based on a fundamental male-female dualism, and that each describes the mutual complementarity and interdependence of the male and female partners.

VI
Monsters and Heroes

ANY DISCUSSION of Mother Goose rhymes would hardly be complete without at least minimal attention being paid to another variation on the theme of duality. This particular expression of basic opposites has been discussed only briefly, thus far, in connection with the Great Mother. In myth these two might be referred to as Heroes and Monsters, or in religion as Gods (or Saviors) and Devils. They are the positive and negative aspects of the Oneness, the twin life-sustaining and life-threatening aspects confronted in Western religious tradition as God and Satan; in myth they appear in many forms, which may be reduced to the archetypes of Hero and Monster.

At the level of the nursery rhyme, these two are manifest in far more modest and restrained form. There is no mighty Jehovah or Zeus in nursery rhyme, and there is no Lucifer. There is no superman, no Christ, no Apollo, no shining Lancelot described by Mother Goose. There are no fire-breathing dragons or minotaurs and no Lord of the Rings.

It should be remembered that these nursery rhymes belong to early childhood, and excessively awesome manifestations such as these are unnecessary. Where there is sufficient inner richness in the psyche, the barest and simplest external symbol will do its work. And where there is sufficient inner poverty,

Kali, copper sculpture, southern India, 19th century

the outward symbol must be emboldened and magnified a hundredfold to make itself felt within.

For the very young child who still hesitates on the threshold of preconsciousness, a small twig may be transformed in play, so as to *be* a pencil or a sword, a tiny baby, a great tree, or the most horrendously evil creature imaginable. This may help to explain why the art of children, like the art in "primitive" cultures, tends to be simple, bare, formal, schematic, and utterly non-naturalistic. It also suggests why, in contrast, most contemporary Western adults prefer richly detailed and completely naturalistic photographic illusionism in their art.

When a tree, for example, lives timeless and complete within the psyche, then the barest outward graphic mark or symbol, the simplest pictogram of a tree, is enough to make that inner tree spring to life. But when the inner tree has been allowed to shrivel and die, then we require that all the richness and visual detail—all the accurately observed texture and color and multiplicity of leaves, twigs, branches, and trunk—be reproduced faithfully for us, so that we may once again be able to experience something of the tree we have lost.

The gods and devils in nursery rhyme, the heroes and the monsters they describe, are so greatly diminished from the scale that adults are accustomed to expect, that they might easily slip past unnoticed and unrecognized. But they do their work in the unconscious mind of the child. Although these two archetypal figures are very closely interrelated, they will be discussed under the separate headings of the monster and the divine fool.

The Monster

Our monsters and devils, like our heroes and gods, represent hidden aspects of ourselves. This is not meant to imply they are not real; they are as real as we are. It is not even meant to imply that they have no *objective* reality. Whether we refer to these figures as projections, eidetic images, compensatory phenomena, or simply as monsters, they quite literally have the power to destroy us, and that is as objectively real as anything need be.

Monsters thrive more in some psychological and spiritual climates than in others. The fact that they are more often described in primitive or medieval settings than in contemporary ones is simply an indication of the greater psychic or spiritual intensity prevalent in those earlier periods. But we do not entirely lack contemporary monsters; Sasquatch, the Yeti, and the Loch Ness monster are familiar examples.

Certainly the most vivid modern account of encounters with monsters is contained in the remarkable series of books by Carlos Castaneda, in which the author, under the tutelage of a Yaqui Indian shaman figure, confronts some truly terrifying apparitions. But, it will be argued, these are purely *psychic* apparitions; such manifestations have no *physical* reality; they are the peyote-induced hallucinations of a confirmed mystic.

This distinction between psychic and physical reality is arbitrary, artificial, and probably obsolete, particularly in a modern world that no longer admits any fundamental dichotomy between matter and energy. However, our long-standing Western cultural bias toward resolving such questions—indeed, most questions—on an either-or basis may have helped prevent us from experiencing the truth of the matter.

What is the relationship between inner and outer monsters? Must the proper psychic conditions prevail before the physical "reality" can be perceived? In other words, is the outer monster *caused,* created, and projected by internal forces? Or can the physical reality of monsters exist without such psychic predisposition? Can actual monsters exist, and thus give rise to the inner idea, the unconscious archetype of the monster?

Such questions as these are probably wrong questions: they demand an either-or answer, and preclude the possibility that *both* and/or *neither* could be true. Such questions derive from our routine assumption of causation—that one thing, being, event, or idea must always come first and cause the next, like links in a chain of necessity. This assumption is now being called into question as never before in the history of Western rationalism.

Concepts such as randomness, simultaneity and synchronicity, complementarity, and the principle of uncertainty are now being routinely discussed by our most objective thinkers in the theoretical sciences, and with as much conviction as they once discussed Aristotelian logic and Newtonian mechanics. Probabilities rather than laws of nature are being described. Nobel prize-winning biologist Jacques Monod deals in great depth with the idea of causation in his book *Chance and Necessity,* and comes down rather firmly on the side of chance.

Simply put, the traditional argument about causation is the classic fuss about the chicken and the egg. Does the chicken "cause" the egg, the egg "cause" the chicken, or is the chicken the egg's way of causing another egg? Or is the egg the chicken's way of causing another chicken? There are chickens and there are eggs, and they are not separate yet not the same. Perhaps it is best to leave it at that.

There are monsters (and there are gods), and they exist both within and without. Those without are not the same as those within. But neither are they separate, neither are they completely different.

In myth, the monster plays a real and important role. Often encountered as the guardian or protector of some prize of great value, the monster represents a life-threatening force that must be confronted and overcome—either through being slain or by being transformed—so that the hero or heroine may gain the prize. In fable both the prize and the monster are commonly placed in some distant and alien surroundings—across the sea or beneath it, atop or beyond the farthest mountains, deep in the wilderness or the desert, beneath the earth. Symbolically, the story being told is the story of the search for Oneness, which lives as much within as without. Both the prize and the monster are its twin positive and negative aspects.

In dreams, monsters may appear in any form as animals, combinations of animals, or in combined animal and human forms, as well as in other less easily definable ways. They are most often experienced as personifications of the threat of death, of one kind or another, and in this connection they are frequently related to the Great Mother in her terrible, devouring, death-dealing aspect.

"And this motif is a recurrent one in fairy tales, where the mother often appears as a murderess or eater of human flesh; a well-known German paradigm is the story of Hansel and Gretel."[1]

The spiritual significance of encountering monsters, as a psychic necessity for transcendence and transformation, is well established in the literature of mysticism, where the death they bring is the death of the separate and personal ego. Serious devotees of any of the various meditational traditions that aim at a spiritual awakening are usually acquainted with the levels of "hell" that these monsters inhabit, and understand that they may be encountered on such a search. The world's mystical literature is filled with descriptions of such encounters, like those of Dante. Christ's experience in the wilderness before beginning his teaching career represents a biblical example of such confrontations with monsters or devils. If the levels of bliss to be experienced within the realm of the unconscious are beyond the imaginings of those of us who are confined to the less remarkable world of waking consciousness, so also are the horrors there beyond (or perhaps within) our dreams.

Monsters are a very real, important, and absolutely necessary part of the psychological development of early childhood. This fact is frequently overlooked by those saccharine, if well-meant, children's publications that insist on altering traditional fairy tales so that the more violent and destructive elements of their monsters are glossed over and ignored. As child psychologist Bruno Bettelheim points out, "those who outlawed traditional folk fairy tales decided that if there were monsters in a story told to children, these must all be friendly—but they missed the monster a child knows best and is most concerned with: the monster he feels or fears himself to be, and which sometimes persecutes him. By keeping this monster within the child unspoken of, hidden in his unconscious, adults prevent the child from spinning fantasies around it in the images of fairy tales he knows. Without such fantasies, the child fails to get to know his monster better, nor is he given suggestions as to how he may gain mastery over it. As a result, the child remains helpless with his worst anxieties—much more so than if he had been told fairy tales which give these anxieties form and body and also show ways to overcome these monsters."[2]

Perhaps one of the healthiest extant psychological practices, regarding the monsters that inhabit children's dreams, is found in the society of the Senoi people of Malaysia. Patricia Garfield calls the practice "creative dreaming" in her book of that name. It has probably been cultivated as assiduously by these people as by any others known. Coupled with a remarkably healthy life-style, it may account for the fact that "neuroses and psychoses are reported to be non-existent among [the Senoi]."[3]

When the very young Senoi children first begin reporting "scary dreams," of being chased by animals, monsters, and the like, they are instructed that these dream monsters can hurt them only if they themselves flee. The children are told that they can control their actions in a dream, and that they must not flee but advance toward and confront such creatures. They can call upon spirit or "dream friends," who will aid them in conquering the monster. The creature may be overcome by killing it or by befriending it. Finally children learn not only to confront and subdue their dream monsters, but even to require a tribute from them, a gift that may be brought back into waking consciousness. "This gift can be a poem, a story, a song, a dance, a design, a painting, or some other beautiful thing. Or it can be something useful, such as an invention or a solution to a problem. The value of the gift should be such that the dreamer obtains social consensus of its worth in a waking state."[4]

To complete the victory, children may then spend their morning in writing out the story

144

or the poem, painting the design, playing the song that was given to them by the monster.*

Nursery rhymes do not present us with many dragons, winged serpents, sea monsters, and the like. Nursery rhyme monsters tend to be much smaller, more intimate and personal images. But the horror they inspire is at least equivalent to that produced by fairy tales in the mind of the older child.

One of the simplest, most familiar, and most often repeated rhymes dealing with such an encounter dates from about the sixteenth century:

> Little Miss Muffet
> Sat on a tuffet,
> Eating her curds and whey;
> There came a big spider,
> Who sat down beside her
> And frightened Miss Muffet away.[5]

In myth the spider is most commonly the embodiment of negative aspects of intrigue, duplicity, and evil. It is usual for the spider to be associated in some connection with the negative functions of the feminine principle,

---

*As charming as this whole practice may seem, it is an efficient and practical solution to the problem of "scary dreams," and has been practiced very successfully by the author's young sons.

as Terrible Mother. In Pueblo Indian lore, Spider Old Woman is a powerful deity whose strength is associated with war. When used in the context of the Terrible Mother, the spider's connection with a web carries a meaning that involves an ensnaring, capturing, and binding capacity.

In the rhyme then, we have Little Miss Muffet, the picture of well-behaved innocence, perched like a little bird on her "tuffet" and eating a bland mixture of curds and whey. She is innocuous, tidy, and every inch a "good little girl." Now enters the spider—a *big* spider—that takes its place right beside her, and frightens Miss Muffet away.

In the form of written language, the rhyme loses a great deal. This rhyme, like all the others, is properly meant to be heard and recited—with all the properly hushed and amplified tones and suitable vocal flourishes, and heard through the ears and the mind of a very young child. Then it becomes a very scary rhyme.

Here, expressed in six lines, we have a meeting of opposites, presented in immediately affective and familiar images for a child. If there is a lesson, perhaps it is that for every Miss Muffet, there is a spider, and the more exceedingly prim the Miss Muffet, the more correspondingly extreme and horrifying the spider. Eventually Miss Muffet must learn to confront her spider, must recognize that she cannot really flee, for the spider is her constant hidden companion. She must realize, as she matures, that the very essence of "spiderness" lives within her, just as there is a Little Miss Muffet who resides in the heart of every evil "spider."

Children of nursery rhyme age enjoy a certain amount of fear and fearsome things, at least when these are presented at acceptable levels; they will even request a scary story. At the age of two, they may already enjoy hearing:

> There was a little boy went into a barn,
>   And lay down on some hay;
> An owl flew out and flew about,
>   And the little boy ran away.[6]

Similar in many respects to "Little Miss Muffet," this rhyme uses a boy and an owl. In myth, the owl has played an important symbolic role for thousands and thousands of years. A Sumerian tablet, dating from at least 2000 years before Christ, depicted a goddess of death, flanked on either side by owls. Greek and Roman writers associated the bird with death and mourning as well. If owls are popularly connected with the idea of wisdom, that is appropriate, since magical powers, sorcery, and wisdom traditionally attributed to owls was thought to come from "beyond the pale."

147

At any rate, the little boy in the rhyme goes into a barn to sleep. Both his sleep and the womb-like enclosure of the barn (where animals are kept) may be understood as referring symbolically to an entrance into the unconscious. While in the barn, the boy confronts the very spooky figure of death, and he flees. Each of us may carry our own death within us, like some indigestible timed-release capsule waiting to open, but it is unpleasant to be reminded of that. However, this is a very gentle reminder, for a child— just the barest hint of the death (physical or psychological or both) that awaits us all within and without. The rhyme is deliciously chilling, because it is expressed within a manageable level of spookiness for a two or three or four year old. There will be time enough later to learn that none of us can really flee our owls (any more than Miss Muffet can flee her spider), even if we refuse to go near the "barn."

There is a modern American version of this traditional favorite that may be even more interesting and significant. Its first four lines closely parallel the original:

Jemmy Jed went into a shed,
And made of a ted of straw his bed;
An owl came out, and flew about
And Jemmy up stakes and fled:

The two lines which follow may be read as a symbolic and revealing commentary:

> Wasn't Jemmy Jed a staring fool,
> Born in the woods to be scar'd by an owl?[7]

For the thoughtful adult, the deeper lesson to be learned in all of this is that the monsters who are the objects of our fear are the mirror-images of the gods, heroes, and saviors who are the objects of our worship. We love life but fear death. We love and desire God, but fear and despise Satan. This push-pull duality of attraction and repulsion, which rules so much of our lives, is one force, not two. Desire and fear are the two sides of a single coin:

> For is and is-not come together;
> Hard and easy are complementary;
> Long and short are relative;
> High and low are comparative;
> Pitch and sound make harmony;
> Before and after are a sequence.[8]

If we peer deeply into the Yin, we find the seed of Yang; if we study Yang, we encounter Yin. Like these, fear and desire are not separate, and yet not the same. Within fear is contained the seed of desire, and desire contains the seed of fear. Where there is no desire, no differentiation, no attachment, and no preference, there can be no repulsion and no fear. Where there is no repulsion or rejection, no fear of loss, there can be no attachment and no desire for gain. The two grow together, and from the same seed, just as gods and devils do.

Gods and devils, or heroes and monsters, are the "outward containers" that are the objects of our desire and fear, and according to the *Tao Teh Ching*, "Those who are bound by desire [or by fear] see only the outward container." The secret of the sameness of the two "waits for the insight of eyes unclouded by longing." Such eyes as these, it should be added, are also unclouded by fear.

The Divine Fool

The other outward container to be discussed is that of the god, savior, or hero. Like devils and monsters, these are found in nursery rhymes only in very much reduced and unexpected forms, and are quite easily overlooked. This primordial figure is present, however, in two forms. One is the archetypal image of the divine child, mentioned previously in connection with "Little Boy Blue." The other is a closely related figure whom we may call "the divine fool."

It has been mentioned that in literature the

figure of the clown, fool, madman, or idiot is frequently bound very closely with that of the wise man, sage, or savior. Something of each of these is contained in the even more primitive mythical figure of the Trickster. Jung describes the archetypal trickster as "a forerunner of the savior," and describes him as "a primitive 'cosmic being' of divine-animal nature, on the one hand superior to man because of his superhuman qualities, and on the other hand inferior to him because of his unreason and his unconsciousness."[1]

In rapid succession, and almost within the same breath, there has been mention of gods, heroes, and the divine child; fools, clowns, idiots, and madmen; wise men, saviors, and sages; and finally, the trickster, an archetypal precursor of the savior. Certainly there are many differences among all of these, but what they all share is a quality of holy simplicity, an ignorance of, or freedom from, the conventional, egoistic attachments, the desires and fears that motivate the common man. There is a child-like purity and freshness of vision common to them all. Like the child in the fable, they are the only ones among us capable of recognizing that the emperor wears no clothes; they are able to see the truth of things at a glance.

The purity of their vision is matched by its intensity. Such figures as these, at their best, live totally within the Tao. Their actions and pronouncements flow from it; they are utterly concentrated upon and absorbed within it. And the selflessness of their devotion is apparent in their passivity, reticence, and humility, where personal credit and honors are concerned. They seek no prizes, and take none.

The combination of all these qualities— egoless humility and nonattachment to the things of this world, simplicity and passivity coupled with enormous intensity, dedication, and concentrated absorption—is enough to mark such figures as eccentrics. They are quickly singled out for their difference from the rest of us, and they are worshipped, or mocked, or both. For, as Jung says, they are seen as both superior and inferior to the ordinary mortal.

The qualities of the divine fool are described at some length in the verses of the *Tao Teh Ching* (as well as in the Bible, and elsewhere). The trait of passivity has already been discussed in the section devoted to *wu wei,* creative quietude or actionless action. Regarding the other qualities, consider the following verse fragments that describe the Wise Man:

On his nonegoistic reticence and humility:

The Wise Man chooses to be last...

(verse 7)

...to do his work without contending for a crown.

(verse 81)

152

The Wise Man will never make a show of
being great.

(verse 34)

Not displaying himself...
Not asserting himself...
Not boasting his powers...
Taking no pride in himself...

(verse 22)

As he succeeds, he takes no credit.

(verse 2)

Because he is no competitor...

(verse 22)

On his frugality and his eccentricity:

The Wise Man, with a jewel in his breast,
Goes clad in garments made of shoddy stuff.

(verse 70)

On his foolishness and difference, the Wise
Man says:

Lazily, I drift
As though I had no home.
All others have enough to spare;
I am the one left out.
I have the mind of a fool,
Muddled and confused!

And he explains his difference:

Alone I am and different,
Because I prize and seek
My sustenance from the Mother!

(verse 20)

In the *Tao Teh Ching,* not only is the Wise Man described in such negative terms, but the Tao itself is characterized as:

> Most perfect, yet it seems imperfect, incomplete.
> The highest skill and yet it looks like clumsiness.
> The utmost eloquence, it sounds like stammering.
>
> (verse 45)

> Or say it is vagueness confused: one meets it and it has no front; one follows and there is no rear.
>
> (verse 14)

Historical examples of such qualities as these are not difficult to find embodied in the lives of the wise men, saints, saviors, and divine fools of almost every culture. Consider three of the most familiar, Gautama Buddha, Socrates, and Christ, as examples of the divine fool. Each of the three was certainly a rebel and an eccentric, if not a bona fide madman, by the standards of his time. Each went about questioning and overturning the most basic and conventional wisdom of his day. Each lived very frugally and simply, and exhibited in the extreme the qualities of holy simplicity and intensity in his single-minded devotion to the truth he had discovered.

Their passivity, selflessness, and utterly forgiving acceptance of others extended even

154

to their last moment, when each met an unnatural death at the hands of his fellows, without resistance. The intensity and charismatic power of each was felt by all who came in contact with him. This magnetic quality attracted skeptics and followers alike to each of the three, and for it each was both adored and mocked.

Yet, in the middle of such intense adoration and skepticism, they went unmoved. Each retained an amazing reticence and humility, and was entirely disinterested in worldly honor. Socrates insisted that, if he differed from the ordinary man, it was in his recognition of his own ignorance, in his realization that he knew nothing. He agreed with the *Tao Teh Ching* that "to know that you are ignorant is best; to know what you do not, is a disease."[2]

Christ was similarly reticent about personal credit, minimizing and obscuring his most miraculous feats, and rebuking a disciple, "Why callest thou me good? There is none good but one, that is, God."[3] All three dressed and lived simply, and Buddha continued to walk through the streets with a begging bowl, even when his reputation was at its highest and kings bowed to him.

Each of these three wise men understood the necessity of selflessness and humility. Christ taught that "whosoever shall exalt himself shall be abased; and he that shall humble himself shall be exalted."[4] It is like an echo of the *Tao Teh Ching:* "If I can be the world's most humble man then I can be its highest instrument."[5]

The single-minded intensity and devotion of each of the three sages—what the *Tao Teh Ching* calls "practicing constancy"—was apparent in how they lived, in what they did, and what they said. They recommended the same concentration and focus to others. Socrates insisted, "I do nothing but go about persuading you all, old and young alike, not to take thought for your persons or your properties, but first and chiefly to care about the greatest improvement of the soul."[6] In a similar way, the Christ taught, "Take no thought for your life, what ye shall eat, or what ye shall drink; nor yet for your body, what ye shall put on."[7] "But," he went on, "seek ye first the kingdom of God."[8] He insisted, as the greatest commandment of all, that one should love God "with all thy heart, and with all thy soul, and with all thy mind."[9] The Buddha also urged that we ignore all personal concerns and "hold fast to the truth as a lamp. Seek salvation alone in the truth."[10]

Such ferocity of single-pointed devotion, coupled with the other qualities of extreme simplicity, frugality, reticence, passivity, and humility, is by usual standards truly eccentric. Such qualities have almost never been admired in the Western tradition, which has tended instead to prize exactly opposite ''virtues'' of personal aggressiveness and acquisitiveness, knowledgeability, cleverness, and conformity to prevailing social standards. The Western ideal of the well-rounded person would never include such reckless and fanatic devotion and intensity as these divine fools displayed. Christ was reported to have fasted for forty days and nights in the wilderness, driven there in his devotion; and the Buddha subjected himself to six years in the wilderness, undergoing incredible extremes of physical deprivation and asceticism, until at last he sat down with the absolute determination never to rise again from the spot, unless he attained the illumination he sought. None of this can be described, by prevailing Western standards, as reasonable or moderate behavior.

The exaltation of such eccentricity has been more commonly known in the East, particularly during the Yüan, Ming, and Ching dynasties in China, when a group of monks, scholars, and amateur artists actively cultivated such qualities, both in their lives and in their art. The similar and related movement of Zen Buddhism in Japan contributed to the development of some wonderful examples of the divine fool. A portrait of one such ''fool'' was painted by another (see illustration). Both the subject and the execution of the work display a remarkable energy and strength.

The subject of the portrait is Daruma, the first Zen patriarch, also known as Bodhidharma. His pop-eyed intensity is explained by the fact that he was said to have cut off his own eyelids, so that he might overcome his tendency to fall asleep while meditating and never relax his concentration and attention on the One. Such fanatical zeal may seem excessive by our standards, but Christ recommended, without reservation, that we remove any and every obstacle in our search for God, that we even turn against those of our own family lest our love for them exceed our devotion to God. He advised no cautious moderation in the search for God, but counseled that "if thine eye offend thee, pluck it out."[11]

In the case of Daruma, only the eyelids were removed. But there is a wise man described in a nursery rhyme who is even more extreme:

There was a man in our town,
　And he was wondrous wise,
He jumped into a bramble bush,
　And scratched out both his eyes;
But when he saw his eyes were out,
　With all his might and main,
He jumped into another bush,
　And scratched 'em in again.[12]

Daruma, ink painting by Sesshu (A.D. 1420-1506), Japan

A truly remarkable feat, to regain one's vision in this way; note that he does so "with all his might and main." The further advantages of such fanatical madness as this are made clear in another little known but wonderful nursery rhyme, which tells of an entire family of such lunatics:

There was a Mad Man,
And he had a Mad Wife,
And they lived in a Mad town,
They had three Children
All at a Birth,
And they were Mad
Every One.

The Father was Mad,
The Mother was Mad,
The Children all Mad besides,
And they all got
Upon a Mad Horse,
And Madly did they ride.

They rode by night and they rode by day,
Yet never a one of them fell,
They rode so madly all the way,
Till they came to the gates of hell.

Old Nick was glad to see them so mad,
And gladly let them in:
But he soon grew sorry to see them so
    merry,
And let them out again.[13]

Apparently such inspired lunacy as this is enough to discourage and conquer even Satan himself.

There are a number of such madmen, idiots, and divine fools described in nursery rhymes, figures who by virtue of their unreason seem utterly out of place in our sensible world. The insistence on one's own ignorance and foolishness is perhaps nowhere better expressed than in the rhyme:

When I was a little Boy
  I had but little Wit,
'Tis a long Time ago,
  And I have no more yet;
Nor ever, ever shall,
  Until that I die,
For the longer I live,
  The more Fool am I.[14]

According to another of the rhymes, there were three lunatics—the Three Wise Men of Gotham—who actually set out to sea in a bowl. And then there is Little Tommy Tittlemouse, who lives quietly in his little house, and catches fishes in what, for other men, are merely ditches. In this, he may be much like the Wise Man of the Tao who "goes unmurmuring to places men despise,"[15] who "wants the unwanted,"[16] and "studies what others neglect."[17]

Simple Simon is another idiot fisherman described by Mother Goose. He is a simpleton, a moron if you like, who fishes for whales in his mother's pail. What a silly fool! Yet this poor simpleton has a twin in the

161

Hyonen Zu (catfish and gourd), ink painting by Josetsu (active c. 1400 A.D.), Japan

figure of the Zen character depicted in the painting by Josetsu (see illustration). This divine fool is trying to catch a catfish in a gourd! An impossible and absurd idea, we would say. But the painting is described as an allegorical description of the difficulty of grasping the Ungraspable; it illustrates the highest lunacy of all—the attempt to trap the Infinite within the net of the finite, a completely impossible task. Yet not impossible for the Wise Man, for the "knight of faith," for the truly divine fool.

Teachings of the Divine Fool

When we ask how such divine fools as these are able to achieve the impossible, their replies tend to be completely baffling. They are either so opaque and nonsensible that they defy our understanding, or so utterly transparent, simple, and obvious that they become cryptic and puzzling. Zen Buddhism, particularly, contains a wealth of stories, parables, and aphorisms that are especially apt as teachings of the divine fool.

One class of such teachings consists of simple declarative and self-evident statements, such as:

The elbow does not bend outwards.

In Japan in the spring we eat cucumbers.

Mountains are mountains and rivers are
rivers.

One is left nonplussed by such directness
and brevity. Our bafflement is increased
when we consider that such statements as
these are offered as *answers,* in response to
very profound and metaphysical questions.
One monk, newly arrived at a Zen
monastery, asked his master for instruction.
The master asked if he had eaten breakfast
yet. When the monk replied that he had, the
master offered his first instruction: "Go wash
your bowl." Such teachings seem to imply
that the extraordinary is to be found buried
within the everyday and commonplace.

While nursery rhymes are certainly not
intended as instruction for those seeking
enlightenment, they too offer a number of
self-evident statements such as these:

There was an Old Woman
Liv'd under a Hill
And if she isn't gone
She lives there still.[18]

In a cottage in Fife
Lived a man and his wife
Who, believe me, were comical folk;
For, to people's surprise,
They both saw with their eyes,
And their tongues moved whenever
they spoke!

When they were asleep,
  I'm told, that to keep
Their eyes open they could not contrive;
  They both walked on their feet,
  And 'twas thought what they eat
Helped, with drinking, to keep them
    alive![19]

  Here am I, little jumping Joan,
When nobody's with me
  I'm always alone.[20]

The self-evident statement, as the basis for
children's rhymes, is not confined to the
Mother Goose collection of the Western tradition, however. Traditional Mandarin Chinese
counterparts for several of our Mother Goose
rhymes exist, and are collected in a volume
titled *Chinese Mother Goose Rhymes*. One of
these rhymes, which deals with the obvious,
runs as follows:

  There's a cow on the mountain
  The old saying goes;
  At the end of her legs
  Are four feet and eight toes.
  Her tail hangs behind
  At the end of her back,
  And her head sticks out front
  At the end of her neck.[21]

Such descriptions of the utterly ordinary are
offered, in Zen, as though they contain some
extraordinary truth:

How thoroughly transparent are the streams
   of running water.
See the fish swimming leisurely!

The dove is white and the cow is black,
Fire is red and the grass is green!

The little nazuna flowers behind the hedge!

These seem to be paralleled quite closely by
such nursery rhymes as this one:

The bull in the barn, thrashing the corn,
The cock on the dunghill is blowing his horn.
I never saw such a sight since I was born![22]

Here, a bull thrashing about in the corn and
a rooster crowing atop a dunghill comprise
the most remarkable sight of a lifetime!

Whether or not there is the remotest
similarity of intent or purpose between such
rhymes as this one and the Zen sayings that
have been described is probably not important. The fact is that children and wise men
alike seem to delight in such observations,
and so perhaps there is something in them for
the rest of us as well.

Of course, not all of the Zen teachings
(and not all of the nursery rhymes) are so obvious. Others are as baffling in their irrationality as these are in their obviousness.
Some well-known Zen koans used as the subjects of meditation by monks are:

Does a dog have a Buddha-nature? (Answer: Mu!)

What is the sound of one hand clapping?

Show your original face, the one you wore before your parents were born!

Statements and questions such as these, common in the Zen tradition, totally defy rational interpretation and analysis. There are a number of nursery rhymes that are very nearly as outrageous, nonsensical, and puzzling:

> There was a man who had no eyes,
> He went abroad to view the skies,
> He saw a tree with apples on it,
> He took no apples off, yet left no apples on
>   it.[23]

> High diddle, diddle,
> The Cat and the Fiddle,
>   The Cow jump'd over the Moon;
> The little Dog laugh'd
> To see such Craft,
>   And the Dish ran away with the Spoon.[24]

In the last analysis, and whatever we are able to make of rhymes such as these, it has to be remarkable that the paradoxical, absurd, and nonsensible teachings in the rich mystical tradition of Japanese Zen may find their closest counterparts, in our Western tradition, in the children's nursery rhymes of Mother Goose.

VII
Summary and Conclusion

CONTEMPORARY behavioral psychologists might tend to agree with John Locke that the mind of a child at birth is a *tabla rasa,* a blank slate, on which will be recorded the experiences of a lifetime. But Rousseau, Wordsworth, and the romantics disagreed, believing that the child at birth is inherently ''good,'' that is, full, rich, and complete. They saw the process of growing up not as an enrichment, but as a diminution of the child's original wholeness and perfection.

Perhaps Locke and Rousseau may be compared to the blind men in the fable, who bump into an elephant. Each accurately describes the part of the elephant that he directly experiences—the trunk, the tail, the leg—and believes his to be the correct description of the elephant. In a similar fashion, each of these views of the child is equally correct *if* we understand that Locke and his friends are describing the conscious mind of the child, while Rousseau and the others are speaking of the unconscious.

It is quite obvious that the very young child is utterly blank about the ways of waking consciousness. Yet if Jung is correct in his description of the collective unconscious, the child does truly come into the world equipped with a full, rich, and complete (though unspoken) language of archetypal images in his soul or psyche. In fact, the child seems to live suspended between these two realms.

If we are able to remember even vaguely the quality of early childhood existence, it is likely to be as a sort of undifferentiated soup in which the separate external entities and events of our lives were blended with one another and with ourselves to form a whole. All of this was flavored by the inner affective elements of feeling and intuition. Our realities and our fantasies, as our inner and outer lives, were mixed. It was not as though each thing and person and event lacked its own particular qualities, but rather that these were less important than the pervasive flux and flow of things, which seemed to meld them together.

Lacking separate names and concepts for time and space, these went unnamed and un-distinguished, one from the other. Places, people, and events swam together, juxtaposed and interpenetrated with one another in a random mixture. There was no clear distinc-tion between subject, verb, and object in our lives.

The development from this partially un-conscious or preconscious state into waking consciousness is a lengthy and very subtle process. It is characterized by the gradual despiritualizing and objectifying of existence. As the numinous light that floods through and unites our inner and outer lives begins to fade, we become increasingly aware of exter-nal and objective reality and the surface par-ticularities of the world of multiplicity.

Perhaps the clearest and simplest distinction between the adult's and the child's experience of existence is drawn in Martin Buber's phrases "I-it" and "I-Thou." The adult consciousness perceives a world of separate subjects, verbs, and objects, of causes and effects, of either-or, in which the "I" acts, or is acted upon by "it," and "it" is anything that is "non-I." The child's experience is centered, not on the separation, but rather on the linkage and relationship between these. His is a world of ever-present participles in which subjects, verbs, and objects merge and flow into one another. They are not separate and not the same.

The first years of life are characterized by a transition from an "I-Thou" to an "I-it" relationship with the world. It has been a thesis of this book that the rhymes of Mother Goose provide a bridge between these worlds. In a sense the rhymes might even be considered our first formal education, if by "formal" we mean a structured, established, and regular convention, repeated without significant deviation from one generation to the next.

Of course any theory which is too glib, too pat, and too self-righteously tidy should arouse suspicion. There is no way that all of the extant rhymes associated with Mother Goose can be catalogued into a neat index, based on the ideas set forth here. The type of interpretation that has been attempted with a handful of familiar rhymes simply would not apply to a great number of others. Clearly, many of the rhymes not mentioned here can not even be discussed in terms of archetypal images or as products of the collective unconscious. Conversely, there are perhaps others that easily could be, and their discovery is left to the reader.

There has been no intent to imply that the rhymes discussed originated as conscious attempts to devise a symbolic body of initiatory literature for the young child. Nor should it be inferred that the anonymous authors of these rhymes necessarily had any understanding like that here ascribed to their work. The fact that some of the rhymes were inspired by actual historical events and personalities is indisputable. But this in no way undermines their psychological validity as expressions of the unconscious. The fact that dozens of generations of children and adults have accepted and enjoyed these rhymes must validate the truth of their symbolic content. Their relevance and meaningfulness is reaffirmed in the unconscious of each individual and each generation that repeats the rhymes, or else they would have been discarded and forgotten long ago.

The initiatory function of the rhymes discussed seems clear: they constitute a bridge between the unconscious or preconscious state of early childhood and the state of waking

174

consciousness that is the realm of the adult.
Both in their imagery and in their language,
these rhymes occupy a strange position between waking reality and dream, between the
actual and the fantastic. The archetypal images the rhymes employ and the often non-
sensible way in which these are related seem
to refer collectively to an original but lost
state of psychic wholeness. They depict that
state and its location in the unconscious,
describe how it comes to be lost, and indicate
the path that must be taken if it is to be re-
gained and integration achieved.

Thus founded in unconsciousness, the
rhymes at the same time chart a path into
consciousness. They gently introduce the
child to features of consciousness: a serial and
linear concept of time; the principle of causation and its accompanying dualities of before/
after and either/or; a world of orderly spatial
relationships, numbers, and letters; a world of
social conventions, morality, and mortality.
But they do so within a context of images
and associations as dream-like (by adult standards) as the very preconscious state in which
the child lives.

Gently, gently, children are led away from
the dark, undifferentiated wholeness and
mystery of their origins into the adult and
daylight world of individuation, differentiation, ego, sensation, and multiplicity. The
rhymes live, as does the child, in a twilight

world between being and nonbeing. Like the child, they hang suspended between the two realms, composed partly of each.

If nursery rhymes are for early childhood, the *Tao Teh Ching* is rightly a book for mid-life, when our worldly and material concerns may have begun to pall, when cleverness and knowledgeability no longer seem sufficient, and when the fact of approaching death is a more intimate reality than it was when we were twenty.

This book also provides an initiatory experience, but one founded in consciousness and reaching toward the unknown. It affords tantalizing glimpses of reality other than the one with which we are familiar. It speaks of a creative passivity that is not dullness or laziness, a wisdom that is not of the intellect, a power that lies beyond the physical. These are beguiling topics at a time of life when one's own bent for action and intellectual and physical powers have begun to pass their prime.

The *Tao Teh Ching* tells of the need for humility and loss, and its message seems particularly appropriate when one has begun to tire of everlasting assertiveness and acquisitiveness. It tells us that "great powers come late; great music is soft sound,"[1] and that is comforting to know when we have grown

176

tired of noise and the powers associated with youth. And for those grown weary of anger and envy, selfishness and discontent, this book promises a contentment to be found in the higher virtue of selflessness.

In some ways then, the Tao is for middle-age what the figure of Mother Goose is for early childhood: an elusive, intangible presence and a promise, hovering at the inner fringe of consciousness just beyond our grasp, beckoning us into another realm.

Conclusion

The purpose of this book has been one of discovery and of synthesis, of finding the familiar within the esoteric, the esoteric within the familiar. This is a process that must begin anew in each individual and each new generation. Each must re-examine the traditional wisdom and values we inherit, so as to construct a new stance from which to face the unfolding of the unknown—which is the present and the future.

In the present time, as in every time, we are faced with the possibility of great dangers and great rewards, but both may be greater now than ever before. The danger is that the two sides of the world may annihilate not only each other, but most of the life forms on the planet—a danger that has never been likely, or even possible, before.

The reward is that these same two sides of the world may reach a synthesis like none that has ever been known. If the "monster" that each side sees in the other may be absorbed rather than slain, the benefits to each will be those of psychic integration within an individual. Two equally magnificent but opposite and complementary ways of knowing—the ways of the Eastern and of the Western worlds—may have the chance to come together and complete the circle, of which they are halves. The contributions and excesses of each may come to be leavened and modified by the other. The Western material contributions to the quality of life may be transformed through combining with the rich Eastern spiritual heritage.

The possibility is one that has been foreseen and described by a number of modern prophets for some time. But for it to be accomplished, each side must develop a maturity and depth of self-knowledge which few, if any, cultures have ever known.

This mesocosmic integration of the Eastern and Western traditions is unlikely unless there is first a corresponding microcosmic integration taking place at the individual level in the lives of people on each side. This inner transformation is, as the Indian teacher

Krishnamurti points out, the only lasting revolution.

The manipulation and modification of external cultural features, such as may be accomplished through organized social and collective effort, provides solutions that are only temporary and symptomatic. Such "solutions" themselves become future problems, requiring further solution. Krishnamurti suggests that the inner transformation, the psychic integration within the individual, is the only real and lasting transformation, and it avoids these difficulties.

The premise of this book is that both the *Tao Teh Ching* and the rhymes of Mother Goose are directed—each in its very special way—toward the psychic wholeness of the individual, toward the coming together of Yin and Yang, of God and man, of the adult without and the child within, of the male and female elements of the unconscious and the conscious. Expressed symbolically in the images of nursery rhyme:

> Gray goose and gander,
>   Waft your wings together,
> And carry the good king's daughter
>   Over the one-strand river.[2]

It is this fundamental psychic integration within the individual that must provide the basis for any broader and collective cultural synthesis. In the words of the *Tao Teh Ching:*

> Cultivate the Way youself,
>   and your Virtue will be genuine.
> Cultivate it in the home,
>   and its Virtue will overflow.
> Cultivate it in the village,
>   and the village will endure.
> Cultivate it in the realm,
>   and the realm will flourish.
> Cultivate it in the world,
>   and Virtue will be universal.[3]

Notes

I. The Tao

1. The Bible, Authorized King James version, Genesis 1.

2. Lao Tzu, *Tao Teh Ching, The Way Of Life,* trans. by R.B. Blakney (New York: New American Library, 1955), verse 4.

3. Ibid., verse 25.

4. Ibid., verse 4.

5. D.T. Suzuki, ''Lectures on Zen Buddhism,'' in Suzuki, Fromme, deMartino, *Zen Buddhism and Psychoanalysis* (New York: Grove Press, 1963).

6. Friedrich Nietzsche, ''The Antichrist,'' from *The Portable Nietzsche,* trans. by W. Kaufman, p. 609.

7. Ibid.

8. *Meister Eckhardt: A Modern Translation,* trans. by R.B. Blakney (New York: Harper and Bros., 1941), p. 127.

9. *Tao Teh Ching,* op. cit., verse 1.

10. Ibid.

11. Joseph Campbell, *The Hero with a Thousand Faces,* Bollingen Series No. 17, rev. ed. (Princeton: Princeton University Press, 1968).

12. *Tao Teh Ching,* op. cit., verse 48.

13. The Bible, King James version, Matthew 10:39.

14. *Tao Teh Ching,* op. cit., verse 7.

15. Ibid., verse 16.

16. The Bible, King James version, Matthew 5:45.

17. Alfred Tennyson, *Tennyson—Representative Poems,* ed. by Samuel C. Chew (New York: The Odyssey Press, 1941), p. 444.

18. Soren Kierkegaarde, *Fear and Trembling,* from *Fear and Trembling/The Sickness Unto Death,* trans. by Walter Lowrie (Garden City, NY: Doubleday & Co., 1954).

19. Huston Smith, *The Religions of Man* (New York: Harper Colophon edition, 1964), p. 151.

II. The Mother

1. From a song of the Kagaba Indians, Colombia, cited in Erich Neumann, *The Great Mother,* trans. by Ralph Manheim (Princeton: Princeton University Press, 1970, Bollingen Series XLVII), p. 85.

2. *Tao Teh Ching,* op cit., verse 6.

3. Neumann, op. cit.

4. C.G. Jung, *The Archetypes and The Collective Unconscious* Bollingen Series XX, Collected Works of C.G. Jung, vol. 9, part 1, 2nd ed. (Princeton: Princeton University Press, 1959), p. 284.

5. Jacques Monod, *Chance and Necessity,* trans. by Austryn Wainhouse (New York: Vintage Books, Random House, 1972), p. 22.

6. Fyodor Dostoyevsky, *The Idiot,* trans. by David Magarshack (Great Britain: Penguin Books, Ltd., 1955).

7. Joseph Campbell, *The Flight of the Wild Gander* (South Bend, Indiana: Gateway Editions, Ltd., 1951), p. 111.

III. Mother Goose

1. C.G. Jung, op. cit., p. 43.

2. Ibid., p. 42.

3. Baring-Gould, William S. and Ceil., *The Annotated Mother Goose* (New York: Bramhall House), p. 20.

4. Ibid.

5. Ibid., p. 17.

6. Neumann, op. cit., p. 276.

7. Ibid., p. 277.

8. Campbell, op. cit., p. 167.

9. Ibid., p. 168.

10. *The Real Mother Goose,* intro. by May Hill Arbuthnot (Chicago: Rand McNally and Co., 1916, 1971).

IV. Myth and Meaning

1. C.G. Jung, *Psychological Reflections,* ed. by Jolande Jacobi (New York: Harper and Row, 1953), p. 15.

2. Campbell, op. cit., p. 33.

3. Ibid.

4. Mircea Eliade, *Myths, Dreams and Mysteries,* trans. by Philip Mairet (New York: Harper and Bros., 1960), p. 27.

5. Jung, *The Archetypes and the Collective Unconscious,* op. cit., p. 153.

6. Ibid.

7. Campbell, op. cit., p. 37.

8. Bruno Bettelheim, *The Uses of Enchantment* (New York: Vintage Books, 1977), p. 12.

9. Ibid., p. 5.

10. Ibid., p. 24.

11. Ibid.

12. *The Annotated Mother Goose,* op. cit., p. 106.

13. Ibid., p. 105.
14. Ibid.

V. *The Rhymes*

Hush a by, Baby: The Tree of Life and Death
1. *The Annotated Mother Goose,* op. cit., p. 224.
2. Neumann, op. cit., p. 243.
3. Ibid., p. 49.
4. Eliade, op. cit., p. 63.
5. Ibid., p. 65.
6. Neumann, op. cit., p. 253.
7. Ibid., p. 247.
8. *Tao Teh Ching,* op. cit., verse 2.

Humpty Dumpty and the Cosmic Egg
1. E.B. Smith, *The Dome: A Study in the History of Ideas* (New York: Princeton University Press), p. 6.
2. Ibid., p. 90.
3. *The Real Mother Goose,* op. cit., p. 40.
4. *Tao Teh Ching,* op. cit., verse 64 (rearranged).
5. Ibid., verse 2.
6. Ibid., verse 7.
7. William Wordsworth, *Ode: Intimations of Immortality, etc.,* from vol. 2, Norton Anthology of World Masterpieces, 4th ed. (New York: W. W. Norton and Co., 1979).

Mary Had a Little Lamb: A Song of Innocence
1. *The Annotated Mother Goose,* op. cit., p. 127.
2. *Tao Teh Ching,* op. cit., verse 49.

Little Bo-peep and *Wu Wei*
1. *The Annotated Mother Goose,* op. cit., p. 93.

Little Boy Blue: The Divine Child
1. *The Annotated Mother Goose,* op. cit., p. 46.

2. Jung, *The Archetypes and the Collective Unconscious,* op. cit., p. 178.

3. Ibid., p. 179.

Peter, His Pumpkin, and His Wives
1. *The Annotated Mother Goose,* op. cit., p. 127.

2. Bettelheim, op. cit.

Jack and Jill and Yin and Yang
1. *The Annotated Mother Goose,* op. cit., footnote, p. 224.

2. Henry Bett, *Nursery Rhymes and Tales,* 2nd ed. (Detroit: Singing Tree Press, 1968), p. 22.

3. *The Annotated Mother Goose,* op. cit., p. 58.

4. Ibid., footnote, p. 62.

5. Neumann, op. cit., p. 47.

6. Ibid., p. 48.

7. *The Annotated Mother Goose,* op. cit., p. 63.

VI. Monsters and Heroes

The Monster
1. C.G. Jung, *Symbols of Transformation,* Bollingen Series XX, Collected works of C.G. Jung, vol. 5 (Princeton: Princeton University Press, 1956), p. 248.

2. Bettelheim, op. cit., p. 120.

3. Patricia L. Garfield, *Creative Dreaming* (New York: Simon and Schuster, 1974), p. 105.

4. Ibid., p. 111.

5. *The Annotated Mother Goose,* op. cit., p. 114.

6. Ibid., p. 113.

7. Ibid., p. 112.

8. *Tao Teh Ching,* op. cit., verse 2.

The Divine Fool
1. Jung, *The Archetypes and the Collective Unconscious,* op. cit., p. 264.

2. *Tao Teh Ching,* op. cit., verse 71.

3. The Bible, King James version, Matthew 20:17.

4. Ibid., Matthew 23:12.

5. *Tao Teh Ching,* op. cit., verse 67.

6. Plato, *The Apology of Socrates,* from *The Norton Anthology of World Masterpieces,* vol. I., op. cit., p. 534.

7. The Bible, Matthew 6:25.

8. Ibid., Matthew 6:33.

9. Ibid., Matthew 22:37.

10. "Buddha's Farewell Address," from *The Teachings of the Compassionate Buddha,* ed. and with commentary by E.A. Burtt (New York: New American Library, 1963), p. 49.

11. The Bible, Matthew 18:9.

12. *The Real Mother Goose,* op. cit., p. 30.

13. *The Annotated Mother Goose,* op. cit., p. 39.

14. Ibid., p. 63.

15. *Tao Teh Ching,* op. cit., verse 8.

16. Ibid., verse 64.

17. Ibid.

18. *The Real Mother Goose,* op. cit., p. 13.

19. Ibid., p. 78.

20. Ibid., p. 14.

21. *Chinese Mother Goose Rhymes,* ed. by Robert Wyndham (New York: World Publishing Company).

22. *The Annotated Mother Goose,* op. cit., p. 91.

23. Ibid., p. 274.

24. Ibid., p. 56.

VII. Summary and Conclusion

1. *Tao Teh Ching,* op. cit., verse 41.

2. *The Annotated Mother Goose,* op. cit., p. 171.

3. *Tao Teh Ching,* op. cit., verse 54.

QUEST BOOKS
are published by
The Theosophical Society in America,
Wheaton, Illinois 60189-0270,
a branch of a world organization
dedicated to the promotion of brotherhood and
the encouragement of the study of religion,
philosophy, and science, to the end that man may
better understand himself and his place in
the universe. The Society stands for complete
freedom of individual search and belief.
In the Classics Series well-known
theosophical works are made
available in popular editions.